In So Many Words

Three Years,
Two Months,
One Me

MARY LOU SANELLI

Author of *Every Little Thing* and *Among Friends*

PRAISE FOR SANELLI'S ESSAYS

"Sanelli's writing is a fine mixture of literary nonfiction and memoir that often, and honestly, examines the act of writing itself." —*THE STRANGER*, SEATTLE

"Sanelli writes with a voice that resonates with readers and neighbors. I often hear about how her topics seem to echo what's on someone's mind, telling stories with wit and charm that resonate in people's lives." —DAVID NELSON, EDITOR, THE *KITSAP SUN*

"I think vulnerability is more important as a service to readers than cleverness. Sanelli's writing offers so much of both." —*PENINSULA DAILY NEWS*

"Sanelli's writing touches people where they live – a rare gift." —PACIFIC PUBLISHING COMPANY

"Sanelli's writing is warm and engaging. It's easy to relate our own relationships with hers." —SNO-ISLE LIBRARIES, WASHINGTON

"Sanelli is an exceptional observer. Her writing is at once intellectually inviting and deeply personal."

—*THE SEATTLE WEEKLY*

"Sanelli's writing is creative, beautifully written, and jaw-droppingly honest."   —*THE BELLINGHAM HERALD*

"I come away from Sanelli's writing resolved to look more intimately at life. That alone is the highest compliment I can pay this excellent writer."

—LAURIE WAGNER BUYER, *THE BLOOMSBURY REVIEW*

"Sanelli brings a welcome sense of the very human. Her essays are communal moments of grace and connection."

—RICK SIMONSON, ELLIOTT BAY BOOK COMPANY

"Sanelli's essays offer a sensitive look at life's tug-of-wars like those between age and time, male and female, place and belonging.'"

—KNUTE BERGER, EDITOR-AT-LARGE, *CROSSCUT*

In So Many Words

Three Years,
Two Months,
One Me

Mary Lou Sanelli

CHATWIN BOOKS
SEATTLE

CHATWIN BOOKS
Editorial & design copyright © Chatwin LLC, 2024

Text © copyright 2021-2024 by Mary Lou Sanelli

Paperback ISBN: 978-1-63398-175-1

Cover & interior design by Rigoli Creative.
Botanical llustrations are excerpted from vintage
engravings and are in the public domain.

The author does a wide range of speaking events. To find out
more, contact Chatwin Books or go to MaryLouSanelli.com.

Printed in the United States of America

First edition 2024

CHATWIN BOOKS
www.chatwinbooks.com

This one is for you, Lou Ann.

*I would be grateful even to know
someone who is as supportive as you,
and here you are my sister.*

Contents

2021

2022

2023

2024

"A drop of water, if it could write out its own history, would explain the universe to us."

—Lucy Larcom, *The Unseen Friend,* 1892

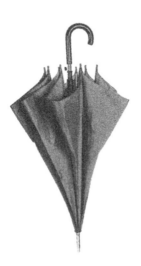

Preface

To be honest, I was afraid to launch another book.

And fear is the worst thing, what it swears we must do (publish), what it keeps us from doing (sleeping), and the toll it takes either way. But having faced the process many times before, I've had plenty of time to think about what it takes to get through it: sit at your desk, brave another day, summon your hard-won confidence, and just keep *going*.

Until it feels as if there is nothing left of you to give.

But not for a minute, not for a single moment, do you doubt how much you love doing the work.

The sheer joy of dedicating yourself to your work.

Alone and absorbed, the only noise you can hear is the *click, click, click* of the keyboard.

So what an odd thing it is to discover that loving the work and loving publishing the work are two very different things. Parts of why this is are still a little vague. Mainly I think it's because success (now there's a word) is interpreted many different ways, but one widely held way is by publishing a book. And if there's anything implied by this perspective, it's that "the book" is the highest reward after completing a manuscript.

But in the real writing world, your first glance at the front and back cover can feel like a terrifying moment when you are scared you won't, it won't, nothing will, and you are terribly uneasy. When more than anything, you want to press your cheeks, which suddenly feel very hot, against a cool wet cloth and lie down.

Upon closer inspection, you even begin to see how *The New Book* is already behind you. It has little bearing on your current relationship to writing. It's hard to believe those pages were ever written in the first place, that you were ever in the center of all that concentration and commitment and now you are . . . not.

I know. It sounds a little deflating doesn't it? Not quite what you pictured.

I'm not saying this is true for every writer, but for many of us the lasting gratification and sense of achievement comes from the act of writing itself. If writing is necessary to well-being (and for me it is), it's the emotional support I rely on more than any other. If fear can dampen your spirit, working on one sentence, paragraph, or page until the words sound exactly right can feel as if you are in the presence of warm light, and throughout the rest of your day, that sentence will cause little pops of pride to keep rising like goosebumps on your arms.

But one perfect sentence—to name one of the best joys, and there are many—is not all that I love about writing. By the way, I use the word "love" here, well aware it is one of the most overused, sentimental words used to describe all manner of affections.

And yet.

And yet . . . I love the way writing reassures my commitment to being me. I love the time I spend lingering in thought, how writing slows down the hours while nothing passes them quicker. I love trying to understand how the big issues affect our everyday lives, how I can spend an entire morning searching for words to express something intensely personal while struggling to make it relatable to others. I love it when something doesn't make sense I can write about it until it makes so *much* sense. I love that once the book is out there, there is not one thing I can do about what people will think.

On that note, no matter how many times I've managed to get another book "out there," publishing still astonishes me with its range of tasks, elations, and setbacks. I begin by envisioning a title, a cover, even a typeface that *fits*, hope and anticipation moving me forward. And this is a GOOD THING. (All caps in case there is any doubt.)

But by design, hope fails to remember the details, too many to speak about here, or the compromises and stamina it takes. While anticipation has no intention of dredging up all the worry and doubt. And neither likes to recall how daunting the transfer of pure writing joy into competitive not-so-joyful keeping your eye on the publishing scoreboard feels, as you try to compete only with yourself for your personal best, but we all know this is not enough when it comes to the marketing side of things.

Last week I went to a launch party for an author who is also a friend. There were several other authors there. (One was sort of famous, which I found a little intimidating, but that's just another lesson in author behavior: whenever a group of us come together, no one is ever totally secure.) At one point, an author I'd never met before stood next to me and asked how my own next book was coming along. I didn't want to talk about my book, and my saying so was quickly accepted. So she told me about a surprising setback in her own writing career, one too personal and mean-spirited to share here, but I could totally relate to how she felt afterwards. "I know this sounds overly dramatic," she said, "but it has broken my heart every day since."

I thought back to a comment made to me that broke my heart, too. Not into pieces, mind you, but a small fissure definitely found its way through. I think he (my first publisher) was actually trying to extend a compliment, but I can still feel the way his words cut into me and how long it took for the two frayed sides of my confidence to slowly meld back together.

In fact, there are many surprises authors don't talk about much.

But we remember.

Let's just say, if there is a gene for not letting things get under your skin, I wish I had it. Because there are things your publisher, your editors, surely the reviewers, other writers, your friends, the embarrassing-under-attended-bookstore-events manager, even strangers will say that can feel like a slap in the face. Even if it's not their intention.

Even as you stand there pretending you are *not* sinking like a deflated balloon.

The last time I flew to San Francisco, I sat next to a woman who leaned toward me to ask if I wrote my book, or did I use AI? From the look on my face, you would have thought she had reached over and pulled a few hairs from my scalp one by one. For all my asserted confidence with words, I'm often at a total loss for lucid ones in awkward situations. *This is a person I don't want to engage further*, I thought, and so I didn't.

But her question made me (makes me) feel anxious in every sense of the word. It's interesting to note that I'd just finished reading a piece in *TIME* by Fran Drescher, president of the Screen Actors Guild. "Everyone's voice is in jeopardy of being replaced by AI," she said, "or being undercut or underpaid," and because her words have festered in the folds of my subconscious ever since, I am prickly about all the AI this and AI that. To be honest, I'm still nervous about algorithm this and algorithm that. How both will affect individual human creativity disturbs me greatly. Just the thought of trying to explain my work to someone who knows so little about what I do is exhausting. So I looked down at my laptop and pretended a very important email had just arrived (you've got to love email for this alone), this is just how the airplane world works sometimes. The trip is only two hours from Seattle, and what with all the emails I was pretending to answer, luckily it went by in a flash.

But her remark was nil compared to a friend who seemed truly put out that I was about to publish again.

"But you have so many books already," she said, as if the thought of it bothered her. I let it go. I saw it as an honest combination of surprise and the fact that too many of us, after a certain point in life, work at no real passion that energizes us anymore, something I'd find intolerable, and I believe this was where she was coming from. More than once she's expressed to me how, after retiring from teaching, she feels more "out of sorts" than she'd expected to. She thought her days of wanting to teach were over.

They are not.

She misses teaching. She misses her students. She misses having somewhere to *be*. With nothing pressing to accomplish, she feels frustrated. And lonely. Her energy and enthusiasm for writing gradually sinking to the point where the prospect of starting a book, something she'd always wanted to do, seems more like a torment than an aspiration.

I tried sharing with her how writers have to motivate ourselves and that energy begets energy, blah, blah, blah, and how this energy moves us along, blah, blah, blah, truths I live by, but, admittedly, can sound a little preachy if I don't strike just the right tone. I had no idea how she would react, but I was proud of myself for trying.

One brow raised, both eyes narrowed, she said, "Well, it's easier for you, you have a husband. You haven't had to support yourself." It was nothing in terms of an insult. It was less than nothing. Even so, I felt defensive, and that is not good, not when it comes to friendship. So I let it go a second time. I wanted to ask—but didn't—what she meant by "it's." But I figured no one ever fully understands what another is going through in a day, now do we? Besides, what could I say? Money has never been my main motivation behind writing or publishing, and no one is more grateful of this fact than I am.

The sun is going down fast and the light in my office nook is dimming. It seems it has taken me the entire day to simply say that there is so much to learn by publishing, and only some of it is about books. Because doing what we love is a good teacher.

And yet I feel as if I have left something out. Something key.

Let me think for a minute.

The sun continues to fade.

Ah. Here it is: If you decide to publish, there is always the chance that you will discover just how tough you are. Because perseverance wrapped in a thick skin is key to publishing. Perseverance wrapped in a thick skin is big. A big, big part of it.

Maybe the biggest.

And guts.

Publishing without guts gets you exactly nowhere.

Now, *that* was a preface.

Part of this is because I have a lot to say about publishing.

Part of it is just because I am me. (And what's so amazing to me, but also so flustering about *being* me, is that in order to publish I have to constantly find the grace to remain totally confident while often feeling completely insecure at the same time.)

And don't laugh, but *another* part of me thinks I need to begin this preface again . . .

So, let me start over.

While the last of my seven books of poems was published, before my second and third collections of essays, and while writing a memoir, a novel, and a children's title, I have been a columnist for newspapers, magazines, and radio. This is where my writings begin.

And why did I become a columnist?

For the money of course. Ha. Ha. Ha. Ha. Ha.

But seriously, the challenge of this genre satisfies me. I like paying close attention to what is happening around me, and in the world, and then shaping my thoughts into something brief and easily readable. I like writing my way through the questions. And like most everything I've ever written, my essays read like a memoir. The world's issues along with my own, this is how my pages emerge.

Nearly all of these writings are new, but the last five have been published before in different forms, revised to allow for more current events. And because Seattle is a place I know so well, you will find some of the essays reflect both my hope and fears about the post-Covid state of it. I've now seen our city go through economic decline and rebounds and enough incompetent politicians, that

I have grown both cynically and idealistically confident that Seattle will be okay. Culturally okay. Economically okay. Hopefully, not greedily okay. Because Seattle has a not-so-good track record of picking Big Tech over the Big Picture, and some of these tech bullies are repeat offenders.

Lastly, two pieces of advice always get me through: the first is to read a lot of the kind of writing that you enjoy; the second is to write what you enjoy reading. Which, for me, is writing that emphasizes what I've always believed: that the most personal *is* the most universal. To know you are not the only one going through something, no matter what that something is, is why we read. It's also why we write. And I am still writing, I believe, more out of discipline and devotion than anything else. To me, success is getting to do this before I get dressed in the morning.

And please. Please buy your books from independent booksellers, not chain stores and certainly not Amazon. For all the aggressive, competitive reasons that aid large corporations, these entities are in the business of squeezing out independent literary publishing. Corporations often begin by wanting to make the world a better place and end up continuing, or even hastening, the problems they presumably wanted to fix, all while amassing enormous wealth into fewer and fewer hands. (Here is where AI comes to mind again, pulling the remaining light right out of this fine afternoon.)

One more thing: what makes me the happiest about this book is that I finished it at all.

On the other hand (since it's impossible to underestimate the power of the word *finished*), I'm not really sure that this book *is* finished.

I still think about some of these writings all the time. Sometimes intentionally, and sometimes they just thrash about in the back of my mind.

For me, this is as close to finishing as I will ever come.

Introduction

In our living room—that is also our den, dining room, and my office—there is a sweeping view of the surrounding rooftops. When I look south, I can see the sky over Elliott Bay shift from a hovering gray to open gaps of blue. Directly below, tulips thrive on stems strong as arms. Without hesitating—without thinking, really—I say aloud to the red and yellow buds (yet to bloom, but I know what is coming): *thank you.*

Sometimes you just have to say the words.

Sometimes you just have to stop what you are doing, look around, and be moved.

When I sit at my desk in the morning, I like to take a moment to acknowledge how fortunate I am to have work that engages me on this level. I do this to counter the worry—the initial worry that the words won't come—so that my mind, eased, will be able to grasp something *worth* worrying about. Eventually an idea begins to push, to fling its weight, to wrangle.

And worry loses. It generally does. And I am grateful.

But after I've found my words for the day, I long to leave my writing behind and be moved by anything, everything, *else*. I want to see people. Talk to people. Embrace people. Even the stock clerk at Trader Joe's who searched the back for another bag of olive oil potato chips because I asked him to. Well, that's not exactly true. I begged him to. The thought of those chips was all that got me through my pages that day. I didn't hug him. But I wanted to.

Personal contact makes a huge difference in our lives. The world is just too lonely without it. During the pandemic, we mourned its absence on a magnified level. Email, a text, Zoom (especially Zoom) is not the definition of contact. Contact is *the state or condition of physical touching*. Even in 2021, I refused to interpret the word in any less meaningful way.

Of course, getting to say this is one reason I write my columns and books. Though someone will likely disagree and email to say, in anger more often than not, how mistaken I am. And I will wonder again: When did we grow so impatient with each other's opinions? Has it always been like this? My mother used to say, "The division today is nothing compared to the war years." I stopped reminding her that we've been in—and too briefly out of—"war years" my entire life.

But most of my readers are far more appreciative. Perhaps, like me, post-pandemic, they relish life on this whole new meaningful level. In so many ways, we have come to know ourselves better. As well as our limits. Which we have reached. Over and over. And over again.

But still, we hang in there.

And if a pandemic had not intervened, I might have introduced this book by saying what I *had* planned on saying before the world came to a standstill: how, as a child, I favored being alone to playing with other kids.

Every so often, I like to remember that self-reliant child.

Especially the way she loved books. How she would hide behind the sofa to read the encyclopedias her parents so proudly bought and then never used, I love that memory.

Later, when I was nine or ten, I overheard our priest tell my mother—I got caught reading during mass, and not the hymnal—not to let me read *too* much because books would "fill my head with ideas."

And you know what? They did.

Books helped me to cope in their The-World-Is-So-Much-Bigger-Than-You way. They still do. I read about other people and what concerns them, and I think, *let's cut all this "divided" talk. We are more alike than they want us to believe.*

Another truth that is constant for me, steady as the sun rising and fading, is that the most well-adjusted people I meet read a lot of books. Sooner or later, everything begins to change about my perception of "well-adjusted" people. But not this. Readers naturally want to know more about what goes on in the minds of others. They seem to understand that sharing our inner life is what makes us most human.

When I snuck behind the sofa to read, I was lost. And whenever I look back at my life, I see that those hardcover encyclopedias were my first interpreters, they explained the world to me much better than I could understand it on my own. From then on, I knew that books would be my future—reading them, and later, writing them. It's just impossible to not be curious if you read books where we are allowed to enter the mind of another and discover so many different ways to see the world, and ourselves within it. And I came to see that *this* was exactly what my parents and priest were most afraid of: In the silence of all my reading, so much was being said.

Lastly, I read somewhere that a writer feels cleansed after sharing certain memories because so much truth has been let out.

Honestly, sometimes I shake my head at just how much truth.

And I am fine with that.

2021 - 2024

"Some things are best learned in calm,
others in storm."

– Willa Cather

2021

Letters, Lies, & Looking Forward

January

I f you want to read something that will make you laugh, or weep, read one of your early letters or emails to your parents. One you wrote, say, during your freshman year of college. But I'm warning you, you may have to delve pretty deep to remember feeling so positively hopeful and buoyant.

I can hardly believe I told such lies.

I was even a little charmed by a few of them, even as I kept hearing my voice in the background echo *hmmm . . . that's not exactly true. Is it?*

Like when I described my work as a short-order cook in the college cafeteria. I went on and on about the free meals, but I failed to mention that I'd gained fifteen pounds eating all that white bread and orange cheese, or that I had to be tested for mono after accepting a second job in the admissions office. I wrote about how one of my teachers was able to get me a "great" internship at the Boston Fine

Art Museum. What a lie. I never mentioned the fact that to be able to work there I had to pretend I didn't resent being an unpaid intern, or how no matter what I said, my male co-worker had to outsay me, or mentioned that I was growing used to this kind of behavior from men in general, or that my boss wasn't hitting on me half the time, or how his behavior brought out a protective, resilient reflex in me. And how I was beginning to see how being a young woman in the adult working world is unequaled in its need to *be* resilient. I also said that I thought I might stay on at the museum after graduation.

I had to stop, read that line again, and ask myself, *now wait just a minute, how could you say such an untrue thing to your parents?*

Did they really believe everything I wrote? Did I?

After reading another letter, I sat down on my bed, stunned with embarrassment. It's funny, but I never revealed that on my way home from the museum, I'd stop in to cruise the aisles of Jordan Marsh, the one thing between the museum and my dorm room that brought a genuine smile to my face.

I rarely bought anything, but I liked to imagine.

My mother saved every letter. And I've saved every column since. And sometimes I feel the same embarrassment when I read one of my earliest efforts. Like when I described Seattle's newly remodeled Nordstrom store as a promo for "grayscale."

I felt so hip using that word. That's how amateurish I was.

Today, I want to tell another story about our country's flagship Nordstrom in downtown Seattle: I have walked through the store for years, and not only to use the cushy lounge. I have my favorite sale racks on the second floor where I dream of wearing a super fancy dress to a super fancy event (someday, one day), and for years I'd stop by the coffee shop for a hard-boiled egg before hiking up to Velocity Dance on Capitol Hill, exiting through the little floral shop just for the scent of it.

While growing up back East, it was Macy's. Pure happiness. I remember gauging my mother's mood by the way she tore through the racks. Was something annoying her? Was someone about to get a smack on her rear-end if she didn't stop begging for whatever jeans she just *had* to have.

I know kids today can't be swayed by something as corny as *Miracle on 34th Street,* but when I look back at our afternoons at Macy's, I can see how they were an easy escape, all too common on Saturdays because my dad was at home and, sorry to say, that meant my mother didn't want to be. Every moment in those aisles was thrilling. The expanse of floral carpet, the ability to try on clothes we couldn't afford, those impossible high heels—they gave us a creative view of the world.

Today, I was shaken when I heard about the senseless attack on Nordstrom's windows. It seemed exceptionally cruel, those boys with their hammers. I don't want to hear the petty details of their collective grievances. I no longer care what they are trying to prove. More and more businesses have closed so what is the point of more violence? There are so many senseless things happening in the world, but I grieve for *our* city. Never have I heard my friend Stephanie—a downtown building manager—say in such a dismal voice, "They just keep cutting us down."

I hadn't been downtown in a while, so when I rounded the corner at Pine, I was taken aback by the plywood over the windows. How could one block hold so much defeat? Gone were the mannequins in their stern stylishness, the reflected light, the passers-by looking at themselves in the large plate glass windows, assessing their clothing, their hair, their attractiveness.

But what is this? *Nordstrom has reopened.*

Reading today's headline, I feel a sense of optimism, an even stronger sense of relief—relief that resilience has somehow triumphed again, and that I get to return to that triumph the next time I'm walking downtown. Maybe the store is full of exaggerated prices and impracticable styles and longings for more, more, more, and the whole lay-out is all about untenable economic inequality . . . but I just love it to pieces. And the next time the wind has been knocked out of me, it's where I'll head.

Just knowing I can go there and fantasize my way through the aisles on my way to the lounge makes me feel, I don't know, positively hopeful and buoyant.

Messy

February

Well, well, my old friend is capable of the worst bigotry I have ever encountered with someone I care about.

And why do I believe this?

Let's just say *your* friend invites you for dinner and you arrive with a lovely bottle of wine and before you know it you are telling her all about the dance festival in Utah you just returned from, how you could barely take in the enormity of so much red rock and open space and how the local students each had three, four, five siblings, so you can definitely see that the Mormon population will grow.

And she says, "Well, they will all be white."

Wait. What? You had to hear it to believe it. Or at least I did.

As T.S. Eliot wrote, "Humankind cannot bear very much reality." And that is what happened to me. I had one of those out-of-body feelings that displaces you from any true sense of time or place.

She looked at me and smiled. But her eyes were glaring. Actually, she seemed to be glaring all over. I could almost see the words, "I have said nothing wrong," written inside a bubble over her head. And that is a very hard mindset in which to Be My Friend. She has said similar things before, but nothing so blatant.

Mentally, I crossed her off my list. There was no reason not to, right?

Wrong. The answer is no.

I would find it very hard to say goodbye. I used to find it easy to equate "new" with "better" about so many things, even friendships. Not so much anymore. She has been a devoted friend in many ways, for many years. And we, at least I, can tire of making new friends. I've done a lot of friendship-nurturing over the years. I deserve to reap the benefits, rely on friends who know me and ones I know.

Or thought I knew.

Still, if we must accept who our friends have become, and who we've become in their eyes; accept the good, the bad, and the cranky—especially when a dark cloud threatens to rain all over our closeness—does this also mean we need to accept a twisted, racist streak?

With complicated questions, there are only complicated answers.

So, you have to ask yourself what is your breaking point? What can't you tolerate? Does your friend's viewpoint have an effect on your own? They say we are judged by the company we keep. Can this still be true, when everyone seems

to have such strong, contrasting opinions. About everything. All of the time.

I thought about another conversation I'd had years ago
with another friend at a time when politics on both sides
of the aisle must have been bothering me more than ever.
I tried to explain to her why, and she cut me off. "You have
time to worry about things like *that* because you don't
have kids." I remember feeling like this a lot around her:
as if my troubles were nothing compared to how difficult
it was to be a mother. Other friends made similar remarks
back then. To them, anything that wasn't related to parent-
hood was less than a real worry and it was practically their
duty to remind me of that.

I remember drawing in a breath, because I really loved
her (most of the time) and we had what I thought were
pretty good talks, even good debates, on the phone when
her kids were napping. "There are just not enough women
serving in Congress," I said, because this inequality
weighed heavily on my mind then, and it is still an injus-
tice I can't let go of. And what did she say? "Women can be
real bitches. I don't think they'd do any better than men."

I ignored her comment because we've known each other
since college and both of us could have hung up mad and
then I'd have to face the immediate future with a terrible
foreboding in my heart and I was learning, determinedly,
to silence myself before things went that far.

And so I reminded my friend that there was a time not
terribly long ago when Italians were not considered white.
Certainly not white enough for how white was defined by

certain New England circles in the twentieth century, as I remember it.

"Oh, Italians are white," she insisted. This seemed to really matter to her.

I was embarrassed for her and more so for myself. Afterwards, I asked myself a slew of questions. *Why didn't I just get up and walk out? Why did I let her pour me a second glass of wine? Why do I still suffer fools?* My emotions got so intense that I had to call my sister, then my friend Lynette, then my friend Stephanie, to talk me down—my island of three who let me be my most incensed-self, without hanging up. At one point I grew so loud, my voice must have carried because when I looked down at the sidewalk, a man was looking up with eyes that said, *what am I supposed to do when I hear a woman cry out?* (Then he quickly—too quickly in my view—went back to scooping dog poo into a little green bag.)

Okay. The reason I stayed put was because of a noise that occurred after we moved on to vaccines, another subject that can become as heated as religion or politics, depending on what household you find yourself in. She has no tolerance for anti-vaxxers who I prefer to call vax-*questioners*. I got my Pfizer, yes, but the truth is, I was afraid to. I suffered the virus before anyone had even heard about it. In January of 2020 I was bicycling in Thailand where people were already getting sick. I believed my antibodies were stronger than a speedy vaccine. And I defended my lack of total pharmaceutical trust by saying, "Remember DuPont?"

"What about DuPont?" she said.

So, off I went in my best know-it-all voice, "They manufactured PTFE resin, better known as Teflon. Ring any bells?" She shook her head.

"$16.5 million settlement with the EPA." I tell this story a lot, so the rest rolled out in one long sentence. "The company knew all along that it was bad for you, and it happens too often: a publicly traded company holds the patent on a product that they know causes health problems, but they *also* know they stand to make millions, possibly billions, so they go ahead with it and bury the reports or hire their own scientists to write the reports and push out another false narrative the media eagerly spreads, and this may be hard to believe, but it's true."

This brought a sigh from her.

"So, really, it's our job to question everything," I said. "Like your crazy bigoted views. How will they ever make the world a better place?"

Brushing off my question with a wave of her hand, she sat, took a sip of wine, her eyes narrowing, her hand rising to sweep aside a strand of bright blonde hair. And then she stuck out her tongue and made that neighing noise, like a horse makes with its lips when you hold out an apple.

You can picture it between two longtime friends, can't you? That sound.

But I heard something else, too. Love, maybe. Or whatever cliché-ridden thing you want to call it when you know someone accepts *all* of you. Even in the face of conflict and disagreement; even in the face of disapproval, horror, and dislike.

So in the wake of that sound—and the less tolerable echo of bias and prejudice—I felt my aversion give a little. It is hard to know when we should argue a point with friends, which is difficult, or back off completely, which is even more difficult (for some of us). But change has never come quickly as a stream of protest images on the internet. It's more about persistence and vigilance, rather than finding fault and finger-pointing. And hating, especially hating. There will be many—I fear too many—times ahead when I will talk myself blue in the face about what some people believe and not one of them will listen.

The same can be said about most of us. I have a neighbor who still thinks I am crazy, a real nutcase, to believe Obama wasn't born in Kenya. Or that Trump hasn't been sent by God to save us from the "elitists."

Therefore, I will handle going forward into this friendship with intent. Even if I know there are messy times ahead, times when I will feel graceless as a trapped dog in her company. Angry as a pit bull.

Angrier.

But you do not change someone's mindset by arguing with them. So every time I see her I will say one thing, drop one seed, to convince her how wrong she is.

Even if she can never be convinced of anything at all.

More, More, More

June

My bicycle was stolen from the Westlake Whole Foods parking lot last week, cut right off the back of my car.

Though what I really want to say (shout!) is that it feels as if my best *friend* was abducted while I was shopping for cherries.

When I first saw it was gone, I felt shaken. Disbelieving. The earth did not move. But it loosened. And I had the weirdest sensation that the asphalt under my feet was softening, making me sink deeper into my own steps.

The first person I told was a beautiful young woman, stylishly dressed, getting out of her car. When she pulled down her mask to say, "Now that just sucks," I thanked her. Words like that matter at times like this. "I did see a man walking around Belltown with bolt cutters strapped to his belt," she said, her fake eyelashes blinking like tiny black fans, unnaturally waving off anything more to say, but in a totally natural way.

And the crazy thing is, even in my despair, I envied her.

It's the kind of envy that can sneak up at the oddest times, a longing not so much for being a beautiful woman in her twenties, but surely more beautifully dressed and definitely younger. When it happens, it makes me feel wanting, almost lacking. And my inner admonition is always the same: *Stop it! Stop it right now! You have so much to be grateful for!*

I stood there struggling in my state of contrasts: Tough, resilient woman vs. wanting to kneel down and cry like a baby about my bike, my sparse eyelashes, my sweatpants.

But I held it together. It was rough, but I slowly came back to myself.

What gets me is I hardly ever shop at Whole Foods. To me, that part of town, South Lake Union, is a nowhere land. I pulled in because my friend's text read "CHERRY SEASON!", accompanied by a photo of three green berry baskets full of cherries sitting on her counter. Any excuse to post an image (six words that could be her middle name), but I had to admit, the cherries looked worth stopping for.

South Lake Union once served as a catchment for logs on their way to be milled, but now I get the feeling it serves as a catchment for anyone needing to steal something quick—bicycles, cell phones, handbags—and head on back to wherever they can fence them. And since this has happened to me twice in the area, I knew it could happen again, quick-as-a-flash, but I pulled in anyway before heading down to the ferry because I'd just taught a dance workshop on Capitol Hill, and I was hungry.

I could just kick myself now.

The first time it happened, I was getting my hair trimmed at a salon in Westlake, and in came a man who scooped up an entire shelf of hair products and ran out. I heard my hairdresser say, "It's not even worth calling the cops anymore."

I won't call the cops about my bicycle, either. Though I should, to get a case number anyway. We should all take advantage of the right to call the police. It's like voting.

But come on. We all know that bicycle theft is no longer something to call the police about in Seattle at this point in time. I think the same could be said about any major American city.

If you go to websites and apps like eBay, you'll see plenty of bikes for sale. And if you happen to see yours, you *can* contact the police, and consider yourself lucky, blessed, if they actually rescue your bike.

In the meantime, I will be glad that the rest of my life is going well and (try to) stop mourning my old bike and buy a new one. Or new to me anyway, as I'm a great fan of recycled bicycle shops.

But wait a minute, where do they get their bicycles?

So I called the store manager of Recycled Cycles on Boat Street, David. Now, taking a phone call in a bicycle shop on a sunny Saturday in Seattle is a good deed by anyone's measures, but he is just the nicest, most positive guy, like a rockstar to the bicycling community, and his reply was concise and upbeat. "We never pay cash for bikes," he said, "that attracts the dark side. Nor do we accept any bike that's been spray painted. All serial numbers are run through the Bike Index. Anything that feels remotely shady, we say no thank you."

People get things stolen all the time, my husband points out, but in a soothing tone, like he is talking someone off a ledge, and I suppose he is. I really miss my bike.

As a kid, if I believed in anything, it was bike riding. Even then I sensed how riding is the perfect give-and-take. The steadiness it teaches is all about balance. And when you master that, you keep moving forward. Too, riding was my first independence. I can still remember the exhilaration I felt peddling out of my neighborhood, past the concrete plant where my dad worked, and into the next newness down the road. Inhaling the sense of freedom, the world opened up to me. And once you get a sense of freedom, you want more, more, more.

I've felt most like myself on a bicycle ever since.

I know most people look upon bicycle riding as a leisure activity and not as a necessity, but riding is basic to my life.

And *this* bike, she (yes, she) was like a favorite cat or dog; she entered my life at a particular low point and affected me in ways no other bicycle ever had.

I just hope the person who stole her doesn't leave her out in the rain. She hates that. Her chain gets rusty, and her frame starts to corrode.

So, thief? Care for her. If you do, she will provide the best equilibrium you will ever know.

And that's a steady relationship, no matter what.

Also, a Beginning

July

A dvance copies of my book sit on my publisher's desk. I pause for a moment, tug involuntarily at my earlobe, take a step closer. "Wow!" I say. "They're perfect."

He sighs deeply, as if even his lungs won't accept the idea of "perfect." Because there is always more to do, more to correct, more to promote, and I get all that, but at the moment I want to run across the street to the cozy little wine bar and order champagne.

This is exactly why I love having these meetings with my publisher: he gives me the business side of things. It's also why he doesn't much like having these meetings with me. Because I don't fully understand the business side of things.

I do understand how important it is to celebrate, though. And that's what I say to him.

"I wish I could," he says, sighing again.

I laugh because this is a familiar place between us— the same place we've been before, and the same place we will be again, until one of us backs off to give us both more room, so it doesn't unnerve me like it once did. There are occasions when you question whether it's appropriate to ask someone to celebrate with you. Maybe this is one of them.

So I pick up the book, thumb through the pages, careful to avoid specific sentences, exact words. I have a sudden fear that no one will want to read *every little thing* (also the book's title, which now sounds sort of funny, but at the time, definitely not) I've had to say for the last five years. But I remind myself there is no going back. It's the end of a chapter.

But like all endings, also a beginning.

And why we call it a *launch*.

I clearly remember the day I finished the manuscript. I sat reading and rereading the last page and by then not one sentence made any sense and I had to walk outside three times before I finally pressed SEND. *And that's that,* I thought. *Finito.* I stared and stared at the screen and when I finally got up, I ran the tub and sat on the edge adding drops of lavender oil until, submerged in my favorite private place, I was ready to admit that I'd just released all I have to give.

Who was it that said that it is only in the giving that we receive? I agree.

Or I *want* to agree.

The thing about receiving, though, is that no matter what anyone thinks or says about your work, once it's bound between two covers there is really nothing *to* receive. It's like trying to receive a ray of light—it's not really ours to catch. All we can do is reflect the comment back with a smile on our face (hopefully), our ego in check (more hopefully), and our composure as calm as before the statement was made (most hopefully).

In another time, in what feels like another era, my first novel was published in the fall of 2019, *The Star Struck Dance Studio of Yucca Springs.* Fun title, right?

Well, that's what I thought. But by March 2020, it sounded like way too much fun in an otherwise unbelievably dark and depressing year. The story is about a dancer who finds the compassion to forgive his homophobic attacker, but even so, in every possible way, the book became irrelevant overnight.

But *before* it did, I was in full swing, teaching dance in every corner of the globe, so that in January 2020, I was in Thailand where I caught Covid before anyone back home knew how those two chilling syllables would change everything for everyone.

It was bad.

I spent the worst of it on a floating raft/hotel room on the Chao Phraya River. It was an awful place to be sick, not only because the rocking made me queasy, but because the bed was hopelessly far from the bathroom. I remember trying to feel my way to the tiny sink, holding on to the wall and wondering if I'd ever be well enough to leave the room, let alone Thailand. Three days later my fever broke, and I remember the release—the heat hissing out of me, the wet sheets sticking to my legs, the sound of rushing water suddenly penetrating the room. It was there all along, but

I couldn't hear it before. A huge plastic bag floated down the center of the river. It's amazing to me how distinctly I recall that bag now.

Another book sits on my publisher's desk, too: Madeleine Wilde's *Notes from the Garden*. Madeleine (no longer with us) was a columnist for one of the papers I still write for. Now, I like any writing that conveys what matters most to another, and gardening meant everything to Madeleine.

I know that a reader may come to our books because of a beautifully designed cover, but they stay for the writing. I wonder if Madeleine, upon seeing *her* new book—its cover, its typeface, its illustrations—would have felt as I do, both thrilled and saddened; accomplished and disoriented.

I feel a little disoriented.

I know sound carries in the garden. So, standing in my container garden on my tiny balcony, I crane my neck to hear what Madeleine might say. It was minutes and minutes later. Almost twenty. I could have just gone back inside, but somehow that would have seemed rude, like walking out in the middle of someone's performance.

So I waited.

And then, as if asking herself the same questions and feeling the same confusions, Madeleine strolls out into her garden to say, "Take note, fellow writer: Achieving your dreams spares you nothing."

Sing It, Sinatra!

September

Would it have made a difference if I had known what was to become of my old neighborhood?

Because I often understand something rationally, but it doesn't change the way I *feel* about it, much as I try. Would I have moved away from downtown Seattle earlier, lessened my attachments to it sooner, if I had known what was next? Or how fast it was coming? Starting off gradually, but then snowballing.

These are the thoughts that haunt me as I walk back to my old place on Vine Street under a September sky that is golden above the monorail this time of the year. The fires still burn in Eastern Washington. There is a faint smell of ash in the air.

It's been almost a month since I returned.

On my way, I pass the nearly naked man who makes his home in the abandoned doorway of what was once the Lusty Lady Strip Club. The irony doesn't escape me.

Broken glass is scattered everywhere as if smashed in a rage, evidence that a camp can turn from passive to brutal in the blink of an eye. The flap of his tent wafts upward in the slight wind. He couldn't look more fragile. He scowls as if there is something wrong with me for noticing him.

I take his scowl to heart. I let it sink in.

Something about his eyes remind me of my first serious boyfriend who was killed in a car accident on his twenty-first birthday. It seemed inconceivable that he could die. Dying was not part of our young plans. Did I cry hysterically? I can't remember. Was I inconsolable? I can't remember that, either. Time has faded the details. But I remember how much easier it was to let go of grief then. It took only days for me to meet his death head-on, make peace with it, and live on with hope and eagerness.

It's not quite so easy these days.

It can take months, years, for the tight knot of grief in my stomach to work loose. When I lost my dance partner, Charles, I cried almost daily for a year. The most lasting image I have of those days is of refusal. My mind couldn't accept what had happened. Denial hung over my dance studio like a raincloud ready to release, the pressure building . . . and then tears again.

Wrapping my sweater close around my shoulders, I crossed to the Seattle Art Museum side of the street where the Hammering Man still pounds. I thought, *you remind me of our city council. You keep pounding but nothing gets done. Businesses keep closing.* And because frustration can give in to anger in the space of a breath, I continued:

Bezos—pound him, why don't you? Imagine the mental health or addiction facilities he could have built with 5.5 billion instead of flying off to the edge of space. I also was aware of the fact that I was scolding a statue.

I do love Seattle.

But it's become an uneasy love.

I just can't seem to love it without shaking my head anymore. Downtown is despairing—there isn't a better word to describe it. I look around at all of the new tents strewn around the city, and I see that throwing money at homelessness doesn't get us far. Nor does blaming. Nor does misdirected compassion, because compassion isn't always what it seems. My question always becomes: other than fentanyl dealers, who is profiting from all of this misery? Is it best to continue to hope for a turnaround of leadership, or cross downtown off my list as simply "too depressing" like so many others have done.

Mentally, I make a case for both sides.

When King County bought the Queen Anne Inn to run as "supportive housing," my friend Lisa hoped for the best. But her beloved neighborhood was quickly overrun by crime, drug use, and violent assaults. She started to pack.

But it's hard to make a new life, new connections, new friends. It's really hard.

I've always been moved by the beauty of Seattle, the clear sea and mountain views, yet now I am fearful, which is a feeling incompatible with beauty. "The inescapable longing for something you never had," as Sontag wrote, is a longing I think I may suffer from.

But *no*. That's not it. Because I did have a neighbor-hood I loved. Neighbors I loved. Business owners I knew by name. They are mostly gone now, moved out of the city because of this same fear we can't outrun, and it's not of Covid. It's of a city council that claims to be compassion-ate—a claim that feels far from the truth. Where is their compassion for all the people who no longer feel safe in the neighborhoods they helped create?

I read that a shark has to keep moving forward in order to breathe, to keep forcing water through its gills. The words struck like a wake-up call.

It's rare that policy makers live in the neighborhoods they govern. I can only hope (and pray and vote) that ours will finally admit that the homeless issue has worsened, in large part, because of Seattle's very own too-permissive public policies. It's time to close the huge gap between what is naïve ideology, and what actually *works on the street*. And it's time to admit another truth: It's nearly impossible to help those who won't help themselves, no matter how much money we spend trying. Or like a shark caught in a trawl net, we will slowly go under.

My father used to sing Sinatra songs softly to himself. I keep him close by playing the songs, songs like "I've Got You Under My Skin." The last time I listened to it, there were a few lines that really spoke to me, so I looked up the lyrics and read through them, highlighting my favor-ite words. Of the many, I like one message in particular because, when it comes to running a city, there is no better advice than to use our mentality. *To wake up to reality*.

Jay's Wedding

October

I can always tell when my husband is thinking about work. He gets this look, this *focused* look, before an added measure of silence travels through the walls of our home—or in this case, our hatchback—to reveal that the man is now as far away as a nearby person can be.

All other sounds disappear.

All other sounds meaning *me*.

So, naturally, he doesn't respond when I mention the dark clouds forming over Eastern Washington, where we are headed to celebrate our friend Jay's wedding. It worries me to look at those clouds, so I stare at my feet, my thoughts reverting to the bride.

It was me who introduced Jay to her first husband, a man who turned out to be, in her words, "a real piece of work." Just remembering how much tension there was in their marriage can still send a stab of guilt to my middle. Photographs from that time show Jay smiling, always smiling, determined to believe that everything would be alright.

And if life were fiction, it might have been. After their last fight, he would have stormed out to the family SUV, sat there for a while listening to the Seahawks game, and then walked back into the house to make-up. My husband would do that.

Instead, he flew to Chicago to live with his mother and never once paid child support for the three kids he left behind.

So, no, everything was not alright.

Not alright more than any other not alright marriage I've ever known. If I had to think of a likeness, their marriage was like two people seeing the road ahead strewn with shards of glass and driving forward anyway, speeding along at a brisk seventy, as if their eyes couldn't adjust. It made me realize that once you've lost respect for one another, you are never going to get it back, no matter how badly you want it back.

When they first met, I remember thinking that because they were instantly attracted to each other, they'd make a great couple, if for no other reason than I always want life to be more romantic—so why wouldn't mutual attraction bring them all the good things we see in the movies and read about in books?

Possibly why my dad told me that I watch too many movies and read too many books.

He's not wrong. But I've watched and read plenty of stories about disastrous marriages, too. But we were younger then and still needed to tamp down, if not extinguish, all thoughts of a failed marriage. In the minds of most of us—despite the statistics, despite the rising social acceptance—there's still nothing as sad as love that has failed.

But Jay, our Jay, is reaching for love again. Reaching for trust. Reaching for a man she says is "a good one this time." She is brave.

Braver still to plan an outdoor wedding.

We are directly under the clouds when I look up and yell, "All right now, you have to hold on. You cannot rain on Jay's wedding! No fucking way!" Now, *this* my husband hears. He can't help his raised-by-schoolteachers innate disapproval of "that word." Even when the likelihood of rain hangs in the air louder than any silence, louder than any cuss word yelled at the top of any lungs.

Sure enough, we hit rain.

First it spat at the windshield, then silvery drops jumped off the roof. How could this happen? After months of intense heat and wildfires burning?

They say a rainy wedding is good luck, but, honestly, everyone's enthusiasm was deflating fast. So the champagne began to flow faster and faster, until a few of us thought, *hey, it's only rain, let's dance!*

I took only one photo of the bride and groom, but it was a good one, and it was enough. No photo can pin down the joy of the moment we wind up missing because we are too busy taking photos. I turned off my phone, threw it in my purse, and felt remarkably gratified by its absence. I was free from having to pay attention to photo

"opportunities," and with that comes more of an appreciation of everything else.

Over by the pie table (Jay's weakness is pie, not cake, so
everyone was asked to bring a pie), the conspiracy theo-
rist among us was saying something about how "they will
try to take away our guns next." There are moments when
everything around you grows suddenly shaded and still.
Tipsy me, I go and foolishly quote the numbers I know:
More than 49,000 Americans died from gun violence last
year, and this year we have experienced the biggest rise in
murder since the start of national record-keeping in 1960.
I'm not surprised to hear myself say all this. Facts are *my*
weakness. It wasn't personal.

Nah, she didn't care.

Stop it. Stop it right now. This is a wedding! "You know
what? I'm headed back to the mud," I say. Which sounds, I
know, like a funny thing to say about a dance floor, but in
this case it was literally true, and the music reminded me how
distant I've grown from dancing with others simply for fun.

I went back to the dancers and hugged one of them who
was moving as if life had never been so enjoyable. Smart girl.

There can be no resisting the music at a wedding. No
one alive can keep me from dancing.

Because dancing always makes me feel good and it
makes me laugh. And I need that. We all need that. We've
had enough of the other.

Because we have come to Jay's wedding to celebrate.

Because Jay is in love.

Because I had nothing to do with it this time.

This I Can Do

December

As one year ends and a new one begins, there are sparks of hope.

These sparks may be emotional or symbolic, but either way, *sparks*. And sparks are many things, but they always shed light.

And that's what we want, isn't it, to see our way into the light? To feel more confident because we are doing something, just one little thing, to move beyond our mistakes. Because confidence is fragile, such a fragile thing. Confidence can fall faster than we think—too fast.

I feel my stomach clench.

Okay, my most recent worst-mistake involved a little too much wine (on my part) and a little too much anger about political differences (on his). But even if I am proud of my response at the time, it will still feel more like a lapse in judgment at 3 a.m., when I'll wake with a start and proceed to scold myself, *you could have just thanked him and quietly walked away.*

But, like I said, new hope!

There are days, like today, when I see so clearly how being a visiting dance teacher has given me new perspectives on everything this man was trying to explain to me.

See, even the most rundown town can have a ballet studio. And the thing that is so troubling to me is how rundown much of our state, much of our country, *is*. There is no inherent shame in this, but it had the lasting effect of abolishing any lingering naïve cliché in my head about the equality of progress, of my faith in it, of the likelihood of it, or any possibility of thinking our economy is on the right track for most of us.

Rundown is not naïve. Rundown is not progress.

On my last teaching tour, I'd anticipated seeing a few towns that are down on their luck, but I didn't think there would be so many, which is really how it is out there. There are exceptions, college towns like Ellensburg. And Walla Walla has reinvented itself into a wine-tasting mecca, a little gem of Syrah success; triggering investors to buy up surrounding farmland and plow under the fruit and nut trees to make room for more and more vines while TRUMP signs shoot up faster than vineyard stakes.

Why?

Because the next generation who thought they'd be farmers feel left out of the tech-affluent, corporate culture of the coast. There is a sense of despair when the only jobs to hope for are ones that have you filling Amazon orders in a windowless concrete hanger.

This is what I saw, and felt like I understood, in parts of Eastern Washington, a tightfisted resistance to anything and anyone that is perceived to be from "the other side," and not only of the Cascades. As the father of one of my choreography students in Chehalis put it, and not all that jokingly, "You lefties in Seattle are nuts." I knew he meant left*ists*, but I wouldn't dare say so. After hours of approvingly watching an out-of-towner correct their kids' coupés, pliés, passés, and piqués, parents will still turn on you if you dare try to correct *them*.

So I said nothing. I can do that. Sometimes.

But in a way, he was right. Friends on the other side of the mountains are always saying things like, "What is wrong with these Trump supporters? I just don't *get* it."

Well, as of recently, I *do* get it. I can't help but get it. I also get that these same friends don't fully understand what employment-hopelessness feels like.

But those who know what it feels like, *know*.

I flush, embarrassed by how hard I came down on the man trying to explain all of this to me, even if my reaction was more about *how* he explained—it seems impossible that some people don't know how patronizing they sound. Because he helped me to see that there are all kinds of blind trusts that people will put their hope in when they see no other sparks of light ahead: Dreams. Gods. Idols. Mystics. Trump.

Yesterday, unexpectedly, I picked up a *New York Times* and a quote from a former deputy minister of defense in Afghanistan jumped out at me: "On one side are people in major cities who are more liberal, moderate, and educated but have grown out of touch with the rural population.

On the other are conservative rural Afghans who feel neglected by a centralized state economy run by elites." What struck me was how I could have been reading this in *The Seattle Times* about our city.

I admire people who can face up to accountability on both sides, but I don't feel as though I meet a lot of them lately, do you? I don't know why I'm asking you this, except that I want to believe, heading into 2022, that *I* am accountable.

Or more so, anyway.

This I can do.

2022

A New Year Begins

January

January feels more long-awaited than other months because it *is*.

November and December can mean family, friends, food; everything good about the season. But the holidays can also be an emotional ride. And by New Year's I have run the span of my emotional reserve.

What is more, last week I woke in the middle of the night after having a dream where I was standing in the kitchen, and with my hands pressed against my ears I yelled, "STOP!"

And last night's dream was even more upsetting.

When my husband thrashes from a dream, I immediately wake. He doesn't, typically, when I have one, but this time he did. "You were crying," I heard him say.

How could it be that I hadn't heard myself cry?

I laid there in sort of an altered state—three-parts awake, or maybe only half—as the effect of the dream slowly let up. "Did you read *Time* in bed again?" he said.

I don't read my news online. I work at my laptop, so any other means in which to view the written word is better at the end of my day. Anything to get up and stretch and walk around and take in the unilluminated, unpixelated world. The 2022-me will still read as many books as she can, but only two reliable news sources a week, balanced by the opening scenes of *Saturday Night Live*. Any more news—heaven help me—is deliberately succumbing to a nose-dive.

I rolled over. I felt his body move over to accommodate my turning over, his breathing inching toward snoring again. I reached for my robe and walked into the living room. It's said that tears cleanse our eyes of irritants, but wouldn't it be great if they could also flush out the shadowy fears that rise a few hours before the light of dawn.

My husband was right. I had read *Time* magazine before turning off the light. I had finally gotten around to reading an in-depth expose about Frances Haugen, the Facebook whistle-blower (I prefer integrity-keeper) who is the kind of articulate writer that compels you to listen. Which I did. I listened closely. Her findings stress truths within truths within truths. She is scientific and smart and intimate all at once.

Haugen studied what was happening during our last election and in countries like Ethiopia and India, about "engagement based ranking"—commonly known as the algorithm—that chooses which posts to rank at the top of a user's feed. But it was Haugen's argument about human nature that really drew me in. In her belief, it is this system of ranking that is doomed to exaggerate the worst in us. She warns (without predicting, which is really hard to do) that one of the most dangerous things about engagement based ranking is that it is much easier to arouse someone to hate than it is to inspire compassion and empathy. "And given that the internet tends to amplify the most extreme content, we are going to see more and more people who, for example, think it's okay, even right, to be violent. And that destabilizes societies."

It was like seeing my worst fear in print.

This is not just whistle-blowing, it's turning noisy data into something easier to understand. Haugen's research reflects us back to ourselves, exposes how easy it is to con us, how culpable we are, how crazy it is to trust big tech and their sneaky, manipulative practices.

My other dream, the one in the kitchen—and this is a relief—had more to do with how many times I've found myself scarfing down another piece of pumpkin pie because once I learned how to make one, I just couldn't STOP! Why had I convinced myself baking was so hard? Pumpkin. Milk. Sugar. Eggs. Easy-peasy.

Anyway, my sister, who is an RN, swears that tears *do* cleanse us emotionally. And she is very sure of her views, my sister, nothing at all like me, so when she said she absolutely knows this to be true, I knew not to object. I just smiled. But we know each other so well, it's as if she could tell it was a hesitant smile. Even over the phone.

But I've started to like the idea that this cleansing in sleep (and in waking hours when necessary) will help offset the fear I have of one, becoming readdicted to sweets. And two, that we won't listen to the integrity-keepers. That we will carry on as if nothing is happening.

Just This

February

Let's just say you are a good neighbor.

Let's say at least once a day you check on the elderly woman who lives next door by walking into her front yard and yelling, "Hellooooo." You don't visit, usually, though sometimes she will stand in the doorway to share a story—like when she saw the man next door leave the house in stiletto heels and, oh, those heels, those stockings, that dress!—because she likes to use the pretense of gossip to draw you in a little closer. But most of the time she just waves from the bay window. And you are relieved there is no need to worry because this is what you want to know and are happy to know.

And let's say that after the snowfall yesterday and the temperature drop to twenty degrees, you notice that her curtains have not opened, so you bundle up and trudge over, calling, "Hellooooo, hellooooo, hellooooo."

Something is wrong. You can feel it.

So you walk around back, and that's where you find her.

But you don't just *find* her—she is face down in the dirt, lying under the eve where the snow hasn't turned the dark pebbles white.

Strangely, telling me this, you laugh.

I know laughter is a coping mechanism, something we do to deflect discomfort, but still, it startles me. And when you say that she just *loved* her nips of Jack Daniels "for medicinal reasons," you laugh again. Not as if implying that alcohol was the subtext of her collapse, just figuring she must have gone outside to empty the trash or put out birdseed and wound up slipping and falling and freezing to death. "And that's a pretty fast way to go all in all," you say. "She's lucky that way."

I shudder in the aftermath of that image. Every fear I have about falling into freezing water manifests in snow. Staring at a plowed mound of it, I can feel my body sinking, impossibly cold. But I nod and pretend to agree that hypothermia is some new aspect of luck I hadn't considered. I figure there is nothing better or worse about laughter as a way of handling shock that is not better or worse than anyone else's way.

Even so, I don't know how many seconds pass while I try to process how amused you sound.

Then I tell myself to forget the whole thing.

I'm not terribly convincing.

I know from our conversations that you believe we are all living in our last days anyway (but not in a "live as though heaven is on earth" sort of way, it's a darker doomsday prophecy) and that pretty much everything we do in this life—on the condition that it is good—is not done in preparation for the next. Because you don't believe there is a next. Souls are not immortal. No heaven. No hell. Just *this*.

Again, no better or worse than what anyone else believes.

When I ask if you are maybe more upset about your neighbor than you let on, you say that after calling the police, you sank down on her couch and cried. "Only for a sec. Then I just laughed and laughed."

I think . . . honestly, I don't know what I think.

And since I'm so bad at learning from the past and can make the same mistakes over and over, I listen to the voice in my head that warns me to play it calm when someone does something that alarms my every nerve end.

I feel content with our friendship, I feel safe with you, but not always. If I forget certain things, I fear I'm going to cause your usually soft voice to rise with an edge. Like how you don't believe in toasting our drinks and the very next time we meet, I tap your glass, forgetting that saying "cheers" or "salute" is "pagan superstition."

I fear I'm going to keep forgetting, whether I want to or not.

You smile, wryly, when I say that I'll never live long enough to know from Adam all of the different beliefs and faiths and religions that can be interpreted from all the different cultures and traditions and backgrounds, my own voice rising to hide my misgivings about strict religious teachings in general.

Yet, despite our underlying opposition, devoutness vs. doubt, our friendship works, *we* work. This isn't the first time I've had to remember that every closeness is a complicated mix. I never used to think how imperfectly perfect such mixes are, but I think a lot about it now.

And why I want to be there for you. I've been given an opportunity to be there for you, and I don't want to sidestep.

"You know," you say, regarding me with a combination of affection and authority, so that those two words feel important, not just something more to say. It's as if you are finally able to voice something you need to get off your chest. I feel the tension break; I can hear it. "She used to tell me all the time that laughter was her therapy, her *cure*. Her cure for aches and pains, for upsets, for everything. So instead of crying about what happened, I've decided to laugh."

I love this story because, at that moment, your laughter became like a star—bright and shimmering.

Back at home, I stare out the window at the snow still coming down. A girl in an ankle length parka walks by, smiling, unfazed by the deepness of her tracks. The whole view looks like something from a movie set—though probably not a movie about a woman in West Seattle who slips and falls and freezes to death—to illustrate a true white Christmas.

I can't help but think about my own neighborhood where the sheer presence of so many of us living densely together in our condos nudges us to live further apart emotionally, if we want to maintain any sense of privacy whatsoever, and how this way of living disperses the sense of personal responsibility. Not one of us *has* to reach out and get involved.

I have one of those weird sensations when I'm seeing and hearing myself say with a sort of Maggie Smith accent, *No point in dallying around waiting for the perfect moment to be a better neighbor.*

I promise myself to help someone in my neighborhood who needs it.

There is a man in my building who lives alone and struggles with his groceries, and the next time I see him in the elevator I'm going to introduce myself, flex that muscle in my heart, and take it from there.

In Between

March

When a heavy rain falls in September, the effect is soothing.

When a heavy rain falls in March, it's just one more rainy day after months of rainy days and I'm reminded how in-between the month can feel. In between winter and spring. In between new year's resolutions and old habits creeping back. In between life's ordinary rhythm and, *uh oh, I feel unwell.*

Omicron: Fifteenth letter of the Greek alphabet. And now, an infection.

It's milder than the first time I had Covid, when one day I was cycling along an irrigation ditch outside of Bangkok where a yellow snake swam with its head held gracefully above the water, and the next, I couldn't lift my head off the pillow. When I finally felt better—except I don't recall feeling myself get better, one morning I just did—I knew I had caught something bad.

For the last week I've done nothing but move between my desk and the couch and our bed in the same sweats I've worn since day one because there is no reason not to. A tiny world has become my entire world: my thoughts, my music, my books, my bubble. I have no energy to expand it.

Which is not so unlike other winters when a cold or flu made me miserable for a week or two, which I've always attributed to the fact that I teach a lot of kids. Germs are a teacher-downside. Every one of us knows this.

And yes, I did get the vaccine. But I did not get a booster. My mistake.

Then again, my friend Chris *did* get a booster and after testing positive anyway, she took to her bed to watch all eight seasons of *Suits*. And my eighty-year-old neighbor who never stopped taking the bus, even in 2020, is still unvaccinated and has not once come down with "their virus." She wears a T-shirt that says, *THINK FOR YOUR-SELF WHILE IT'S STILL LEGAL,* and she will go on and *on* about the "scam between big-pharma and Biden." About this, her mind is made up. There is no wiggle room.

Luckily, feeling unwell has its productive side: plenty of time to read and tidy. Plenty of time to *think*. It reminds me of learning to swim in my father's boss's swimming pool. How I had to stop trying to control the weight of my limbs, a stability entirely new to my senses, and believe that the chlorinated paradise of Mr. Roncari's new and irresistible Esther Williams swimming pool would support every panicked part of me.

So, stability.

Another word to think about as the walls close in.

And there it is. I begin to feel how the roots of a word like "stability" run deep.

So deep that when I close my eyes, I see clearly how every tree, every bush, every delicate stem, depends on a whole system of tangled roots for support, and so do we. Roots that—for all the intuitive reasons thoughts come to us—work their way into my brain to unlock thoughts of B. (As I'll call her.)

Which unlocks the story I've been trying to get at.

The story itself.

Because B. throws *off* my stability. B. makes me feel like my stem will snap.

B. is the last friend I saw before this latest variant kicked me in the butt—kicked me hard in the butt, is still kicking my butt—so our visit lingers in my mind like a song I can't stop humming. When part of me says yes, I love this song. And part of me says, no, stop. I mean it, *stop*.

Here on this beautiful island, where remoteness can make connection (or its opposite: isolation) the focal point of our lives, we *should* be able to find open-minded conversation easier than if we lived somewhere dreadful or dangerous or where people say polite things and nothing else. But it's always the same outcome with B. I start out trusting and positive, happy to share a meal and conversation because that's what B. says she loves about our friendship, the *conversation,* and I like the sound of that.

But what we have is not a conversation. What we have is her telling me how wrong I am. About most things, most of the time, as if it's for my own good. We talk, but I am afraid to broach subjects that really matter to me. Something I say always needs correcting. I feel the surface wobble, my hopefulness sliding over the edge. I know I should defend myself, but it's easier to go on acting as we are, wanting to believe in our affectionate story.

This last time we saw each other, she was so, so, sure about something I didn't think was true. I knew this even as she spoke. As soon as I got home I fact-checked her claim (she was mistaken, her timeline was wrong, her facts were off), the claim that made her say, "You know what your problem is?"

My problem.

My mouth dropped open. I've been insulted before, but this takes the cake.

People say this a lot, things "take the cake" all the time. I used to wonder what this saying really meant. I have since learned its meaning. There are people who *do* take the cake, they take it and crumble it all over the place where we are most vulnerable. For example: when B. called Ruth Bader Ginsburg "the lizard lady," I let seconds go by. Five. Ten. *It is good to count to ten.* Twelve. Fifteen. Then I excused myself.

The real surprise is how pointed her corrections feel, how deliberate. I'd never want to show such disregard for a friend's opinion (to their face, anyway), but what do we do when someone has no problem vocally disregarding ours? It's one thing to disagree, quite another to criticize. It's something like the difference between a gardener with pruning shears and a logger with a chainsaw. I was caught in a feeling near to grief, but not grief, more of a sense of a separation, of a divide.

That's it!

I thought I'd have more trouble defining us, but "divide" describes B. and me to a T. Like too many Americans, we are divided by vast space. We are two sides of a gap that refuses to bridge, living in parallel worlds, watching parallel news, reading parallel information. "They" think what they think, and "we" think what we think, and we see less and less of each other.

So I ask myself, *What do you respect most in others?* Not a bad question to ask ourselves now and again.

Okay: listening skills, a sense of humor, someone who never misses an opportunity to be generous. Or kind. Or more truthful because they want to learn, not lecture. Someone who can relax and help me do the same. Someone comfortable with love and how to love and *be* loved. I am an idealist this way, I know that. Thinking about the people I love is what gets me up in the morning and helps me unwind at night.

This is when I realize that it's not just the month that feels in between, *I* am in between.

What an in between state I am in.

The previous version doesn't like to give up on people, but the present me knows we can't change anyone, only ourselves. So, after B. said, "People like you think everyone should get along, but that's not how the real world is," I let those words penetrate, and I am still picking out the slivers. *People like you. The real world.*

And I thought, *No. I don't think this is how the world is, but I don't want to be angry all the time, disapproving all the time.* Because that's my real worry, isn't it? The worst of all fates: cynicism.

While we were new to each other, I felt it easier to stand up for myself, my beliefs. But life moves on, and attitudes are changing, and B. is changing, and I am changing, and the world is constantly changing, yet we don't seem to be able to revise our dialogue so that it's not the same old "your side vs. mine," and it eats at me.

I'm leaving out a lot of our decade-long history, of course—the generosity, the laughter—because another thing about Covid-fogginess is that everything feels harder to complete.

But something has to give.

And this something, whatever it is, is trying to connect me with what kind of person to move forward with and who to let go of, and how to quiet the tinges of guilt that will follow.

I've heard it said that half of life is finding love; the other half is letting it go. Which is agonizing.

Agonizing as, say, going through my mother's closet after she died, when I could feel her—what it was like to dress like her, think like her, *be* her.

It was a surrendering.

Also, necessary.

Word By Word

April

I don't dream in images.

That is, I don't see pictures. I see sentences—sentences I can read. Sentences that may redefine how others visualize a dream, but I've dreamed this way for so long, I wouldn't know how to dream any other way.

How these sentences began isn't a mystery. They go hand in hand with my love of reading, usually prompted by whatever book that I am immersed in, and how I react to both the story and how it is written. Once I'm asleep, these reactions emerge, word by word, along a flat black line, in cursive with punctuation—commas, periods, parentheses—in place; sentences that want nothing more than to make my mind a truer place in which to live.

They are not always successful.

They *are* always revealing, though. Even when brief as a single word.

But one word can be a full sentence. Right?

Nor are they new to my dream cycles. When I was a kid, *Highlights* was my favorite read, and mine alone, though I was supposed to share the magazines with my sisters. I didn't share them with my sisters. In winter, I hid them under my bed. In summer, in my tree fort—open to the sky and smelling of leaves and wood.

No one ever found me in my fort, and that's what I wanted. Without intrusion, which I also wanted, I could breathe in the air, feel the wind, and finally stop trying to be someone others approved of. I was eager to know myself in the world outside of my family, my school, my neighborhood. I've always been comforted by the feeling of privacy.

My fort was neat, dry, and filled with the sound of chirping birds. I liked to watch the tree swallows rush through the maples and oaks. When the afternoon sun hit the paper birch, the white bark illuminated everything around it—every tree, every plant, every insect hovering in the hazy light between the lowest branches and the ground. The sound of water flowing in the shallow brook underneath reminded me that the forest was alive, forever encroaching, and ready to reclaim its rightful tree—which, I think, is a perfectly understandable entitlement—and I grew more attentive to the natural world because of it. It doesn't take much to grab your attention, or distract it, when you are a kid alone in a tree fort, and it was about this time that I started dreaming in sentences.

My father was worried. "Don't let the neighbor kids climb up," he said, which didn't bother me, I didn't want the neighbor kids to climb up. But I couldn't imagine what he meant by "dangerous." To me, the rickety stepladder and weather-beaten boards weren't a hazard, but safety. The magic was not obvious to him—no grace of line to his draftsman eye—but I thought the lopsidedness of my three walls (it was more of a lean-to) was its most endearing quality.

To this day, a small home will fill me with a sense of safety. But it's not like this when I visit a huge, lavish house. I don't get a sense of safety, even if "safe" is what the owners are after by installing alarm systems or living behind gates. It's as if I can feel certain tensions seeping out of massive houses, and those tensions will gather in sleepy sentences inside of my head.

I'm not saying every huge house is chaos waiting to happen. I'm just saying that's how I internalize them.

And I know why.

Listening to my parents' marriage implode within the "dream" house my father built, the small size of my fort became, not all at once but as the fights intensified, a safety net. I felt more at home in my fort than anywhere else. And I've been searching for that same feeling ever since. A few of my homes have come close. But most of the time I feel as if my ideal place is still out there.

To remember these sentences, to keep them fresh, I keep a pen and pad by the bedside. I write terribly in the dark and most mornings I have no memory of the sentences. But when I re-read the scribble, I see how the words want to matter, they want to try. They work hard. They fail just as often. But they *try*.

My last dream-sentence said everything a writer might want to say to herself: *Writing is the ritual I found for myself in the hope that my life and my work would always be the same.* I'd been reading Mary Oliver, so naturally my voice was introspective and wistful. But I was thrilled to know how well my subconscious knows me.

Two hours later, the words were harsher. They posed a question. Two questions.

Between dreams, I'd turned on the light, picked up *The New York Times* (never a good idea if sleep is what you're after), and proceeded to read about the Russian invasion of Ukraine, human suffering I was afraid to face, but I made myself read every account; study every photo.

I tossed and turned in the aftermath.

It was around 5:30 a.m. when I scrawled, *How did the world view us when we invaded Iraq, Afghanistan, Vietnam? What about Japan, those unthinkable bombs?!!!!* The exclamation points ran off the pad. I was *upset.*

And I remember with absolute clarity why I was so upset, aside from the Russians, the wars, unthinkable bombs, and all the horrible mistakes we make over and over again: Earlier that evening, at my sister's table, I ate red meat for the first time since I was seventeen. I didn't know I was eating it. It was in the *sauce.*

My stomach didn't seem to notice.

My mind, however—clearly more sensitive—rebelled, leaving three more sentences in its wake: *I've witnessed a stockyard in Texas with my own two eyes. I swore I'd never eat beef again. But it's a small mistake, silly, cut yourself a break.* And when I bent over to read that last sentence, I stopped making the bed, sat down, and let those forgiving words hang in the air like fragrant smoke.

My life has always been about small nests, small pleasures, small wins. This sentence surfaced lately. The words made their way in, they made new mistakes (for instance: I don't like the word "wins"), but they made me see.

They made me listen.

Earbuds. What Ever Happened to Earbuds?

May

It seems like only yesterday I began to search the internet for 100 percent cotton masks. And here it is two years later, and we are still having the "should I/should I *not* throw away my masks" conversation.

Personally, I don't have to rack my brain about this.

I moved to a new building, in a new neighborhood, in what feels like a new age, in early 2021. And ever since, like a detective, I've had to piece together the clues as to what my neighbors look like: whose forehead belongs to what mailbox? Whose fleece vest belongs to which little white dog? Whose face (or partial face) I am happy to see and whose eyes to avoid.

Last night I chucked my last mask because the inside was just disgusting.

The problem with acting on impulse when it comes to sensitive matters, though, is that one way or another you are going to regret it, and during my first maskless trip to the store, I did. The last thing you want to feel when you are breezily going about your business in the shampoo and conditioner aisle is that you are being stereotyped as an anti-masker. I noticed people went out of their way to give me a wide berth. One woman shook her head at me. I smiled. (But I had thoughts that I won't bother writing because I will just delete them later.)

Further down the aisle by the makeup, I approached a woman I know from my building and said, "The CDC order was dropped, but I feel like I'm the only one happy about it."

She waves and says, "Oh, I'm afraid to take off my mask."

People can surprise you. The first time we met, her mask had a cheerful floral pattern that made me hope that *she* was a cheerful person.

She is. And, like me, ready to toss her mask, she said back in March as we stood together under a huge oak tree on our property, watching the squirrels turn over leaves and our courtyard into a captivating stage.

"Oh, I don't mean I don't *want* to take it off," she said, squinting an eye at a bottle of foundation. "I've done pretty well with my eyebrows over the last couple of years, but I've let the rest of my face go. I've been meaning to learn how to apply foundation."

"Which is another mask," I say, and thank goodness she laughs.

"Could they make this list of ingredients any smaller?"

"Oh, you don't want to read what's in there," I say. And slowly, she drops her solid white mask to reveal the worst rash on her cheeks. "My dermatologist told me it's an allergy to the fibers that masks are made from. Did you know polyester is made from petroleum? Because I didn't."

I did know. Early into the mask mandate, I found a website that documents skin problems people are having from wearing what is basically spun petroleum hydrocarbons, and I remember wanting to forward it to everyone I knew, but I stopped myself. People bought gobs of disposable masks because they *look* harmless and are inexpensive, so I told myself—and I have continued to tell myself to this day—to keep quiet about what I know about these fumy masks because who needs more frustration and bad news? Most people don't want to question everything. Even when the truth is in front of their nose, literally.

At check out, a clerk—a clerk who could be ringing us up—reminds us that self-check is open.

Lately, in situations like this, I find myself imagining all kinds of T-shirts I'd like to design. My latest would say, "Dear Software Developer: About self-checkout. How will all the people who don't have a tech degree find work if you keep eliminating their job possibilities?"

Think of all the interactions people have with checkout clerks, possibly the only one in a day. Think of the only job for an out of work college graduate (which was my case) and the only job for a newly married broke writer (also my case). Entry level positions are necessary. Why give humans one more reason to avoid using social skills?

It's a busy day in the store, the line is getting long. And there is a dog doing a pretty good job of annoying everyone, so I turn around to see where all the barking is coming from only to see a woman, mask below her mouth, softly woofing into her phone at a dog barking with joy, as dogs will do when humans impersonate them, so not only does she hear the barking, so must everyone else.

I tighten my thickest shawl of patience, but I feel it slipping. I nearly lose it, but I ask myself if I really want to insert myself into a dog-adoring situation. I know how people are about their pets. I know how I was about *mine*. I talked to my cat, about my cat, and for my cat by making up cute little replies that I could imagine her saying. (Lily. Do I miss you? Yes, everyday, yes.)

I used to like going to the store during the worst of Covid. Unlike most, I *wanted* to be around people.

But now?

I just don't know.

I don't trust myself. I am *this* close. I turn around again and stare at the woman who is still woofing. I take a deep breath. I take another.

The woofing continues.

I want to ask, "What good is your mask if it sits below your nose? Instead, think about wearing earbuds, why don't you?"

In just as testy a tone, I imagine her yelling back, "I'm sorry, I thought this was a free country!" (Also a great line for a T-shirt.) And any one of us can imagine how this confrontation would go in this phone-rude day and age.

When I tell this story to a friend at our favorite little wine bar on Winslow Way, we laugh so loudly that the people at the next table complain.

My eyes widen, I cross my arms (which is something I do when I'm mortified), but we are good sports about it. We stop being so loud. It all lasts less than a minute, and then we are over it.

But to be honest, once it was over, I was relieved to feel so embarrassed. It will help next time I am out in public and need to grasp my patience shawl so tightly my knuckles turn red.

Boundless

July

As a promise to myself, I've avoided writing about public speaking lately.

I mean, you can be invited to the finest group of well-intentioned listeners and there is still going to be that someone who forgets to turn off their phone, won't stop answering texts, or pays more attention to the video they are making—as if they need proof they attended—than to anything you say.

And that pretty much sums it up.

Except a few things happened lately that were so unexpected, that after thinking that it's nearly impossible to surprise me, that experience has ironed every fold of naïveté out of my speaking persona, I realize some things can and *will* stop me in my tracks, even as I calmly pretend otherwise.

For starters, it's still possible to hurt my feelings. I may be better at hiding it, and letting go of it after a day, ten at most, but I suppose I will always feel slighted by a slight.

When that one audience member (and there is usually one) rolls her eyes dismissively, shrugs one too many times, or interrupts my talk to add her own opinion *before* the Q & A, I maintain my composure, but it's women like this that have completely quashed the illusion that all women are supportive sisters. They are not.

However. I should note that certain impoliteness has made me stronger, since no one would stand in front of a room full of strangers and openly share their work if they didn't want to develop strength; possibly an iron skeletal system.

They say nothing is more valuable than a sharp critic, but when people are watching, it's difficult to know whether to pay attention to a sudden critique or disregard it, let alone form your surprise into a professionally-positive response. I've always admired people who are quick with comebacks no matter what—there is something about the authority they possess, but it's always been hard for me to think on my feet. I need time.

I've even begun to wonder if some of these critics really care if they agree with me or not. What matters to them is the argument, and the most pedantic ones seem to want to turn arguing into a bit of an art form to amuse themselves. I didn't understand this at first. I was green. "Well, yes . . . " people like this will say in that way of theirs that always means, "no." I've seen speakers cut these people off with a lot of finesse. One speaker told me to remember that how people treat the guest speaker says a lot about how they feel about themselves. I have to remind myself of this sometimes. I can fix a smile on my face and feign that rudeness is nothing, but it's all I can do to contain my uneasiness and not go on the defensive.

"It's challenging work," the same speaker said.

"I like a good challenge," I said.

And I held onto this conviction for as long as I could.

Right up until my next reading where I shared a piece about what it was like to be seriously ill in a third-world country, in Thailand, and a woman interrupted me, mid-sentence, to say that Thailand is *not* a third-world country, but a developing one, and that I "should check my facts."

Like the pause that happens when you nick your finger with a knife before the blood seeps out, the room sat perfectly still, waiting for my response. I found it strangely emboldening. "Well," I said, "you should have seen my privy. I was afraid I'd slip into the Mekong River through the hole in my floor." A second hush followed—the kind of hush where you can hear everyone's curiosity humming as they try to figure out if they should laugh or clap or neither. Or both.

I imagined myself giving this woman a good old fashioned smack upside the head even if it feels politically incorrect to ever admit you want to smack someone—in Seattle, anyway. My Uncle Victor would have laughed at this thou-shall-not-ness. He knew just how to smack us, the cousins, light enough so we wouldn't cry, firm enough to let us know we were way out of line so *shaddaaap*.

It was a gift, really, his know-how.

Okay, so here are a few awkward moments I'm still processing in hope that writing about them will make me remember how proud I was of my improvisations: One woman in the front row doesn't just sneak out, she stands and announces that she has to pee. ("So do I," I said, and everyone laughed.) Another's phone rings and she answers the call. ("Is that my mother?" I said, "because I know she hates this jacket." Again, laughter.) Another spills a glass of water, gets up to clean it, finds a mop, moves the chairs in the front row so she can mop the floor. I had to regain the room's attention once, twice, a third time. It took me a while to realize she wasn't going to stop mopping. I was ready to walk away from the podium, and I had to work really hard not to. *Is it a lost art, listening*? I wondered. All these weeks later, this woman is still the epitome of how I feel about this question. I don't remember the rest of my talk with any clarity at all. But I got through it.

I have a lot of these stories because I spend a lot of time promoting my books this way, but after writing that last paragraph I want to put aside the worst and remember some of the finest moments. Because there are more readings that go so *right*, when the audience is fully with me, generous at the book table, no one asks if they can buy my book on Amazon, and the programmer invites me back with a hug, and that hug lifts every part of me with its kindness. Readings that fill the room with energy so alive it dismisses any fears I have that human contact will be overshadowed by the virtual experience and that manners are a thing of the past. An author willing to reveal herself is not lost on these book-loving people. Instinctively, they sit up straighter, they stop talking, the focus of the room seems to center around the idea of books and reading—in short, they behave.

When I sat down to work this morning, I had no intention of writing about speaking. But here's what happened: having to choose between writing about Seattle's unrelenting addiction crisis (inspired by my latest walk downtown where I faced several lost souls shooting up on the sidewalk, one trying to masturbate at the same time), or a neighbor telling me that one of the nicest men in our building was found floating face down in the waters in Hawaii, or the latest shooting in Uvalde that is giving me nightmares, or the abortion debate that also wakes me in the middle of the night as I think of all the frantic women driving across state lines to get help they can't afford, so that this year feels as if it's determined to revoke the twenty-first century, I decided to write about speaking because there is only so much bleakness any one of us can stand.

This choice, this saving myself, is part of why I write. It's the part that holds me together through the worst of it as I stumble my way into my writing for the day, after being pushed not by one thing, but by everything.

And if I were to *be* that push today, I would say: *Speaking may be a personal topic, but it's going to take center stage today and give you the opportunity to look back on the work you do with both wonder and thanks.*

There are mornings when my appreciation of this push is boundless. When I pay even closer attention to what is in front of me. Mornings when I lose myself in something frivolous so that I won't lose the thread of humor, the lifeline.

And for hours, the world's troubles seem to disappear. Almost.

Islands

July

In the years before now, those days before semi-automatic rifles made going to school—a parade, a church, a market, a mall—a terrifying decision and a testament to political gridlock; in the years when my extended family got together on Sundays to eat food slow-cooked over low heat; when most of us followed basic social etiquettes instead of excessive social media (and I hadn't yet fallen behind on most of it because I am social media'd *out*); in those years before acronyms passed for communication and emojis for interaction, I began my first book.

I didn't *know* I was writing a book.

Introduced to writing by my favorite college professor, a feminist from Texas who let her gray hair flourish in her thirties instead of becoming honey blonde for the rest of her middle age, it was in her Boston classroom, four flights of stairs over Commonwealth Avenue, that I realized my writing didn't have to say anything profound—a relief, since I hadn't yet done anything profound—it was more about the *way* a sentence is written.

The doors to my imagination opened wide that year. I peered inside. I started writing.

Soon after, on a Greyhound bus, I moved from the East Coast to the West. Towns and prairies and deserts slipped by, and my first poems grew into a collection. But again, I didn't know I was writing a collection. I knew only that, more than anything or anyone, those poems helped me adjust to my new coast.

And I called it a "coast," but I knew it wasn't at all the same sort of "coast" I left behind.

I grabbed my backpack from under the bus in the station at Eighth Avenue and Stewart and pushed out the doors into the cool marine air. The bus station looked the same as all the others along the way, stations always look the same, but as soon as I made my way down to the waterfront to cross Puget Sound on a ferry that divides one way of life from another, I could hardly believe I'd found such a safe, green, place.

That first ferry ride still moves me—the sheer, fluid, fact of it.

And I think of it now because I'm on another ferry, this one to Orcas Island. It's the perfect summer day. The sky is cloudless. The sun blasts my eyes, but I keep staring at it anyway. Rosario Strait is calm. There's a breeze but it's not windy. Overhead, there is a low-flying private jet and I search the sky for others the way I look for eagles. "There's a Learjet," I say to no one in particular, and my seatmate corrects me. "It's a Gulfstream," he says, "no one flies Lear's anymore," and all I can think is: *I've also fallen behind on the personal aircraft of the ultra-wealthy. Sorry.*

I've only met one man with his own jet, ever. He was much older than his wife, and I met them both on the island of Kauai, where, at a restaurant in Princeville, she asked me about the basket I was carrying with eyes that reflected what I thought was interest. Or curiosity, possibly. So I started to say how the basket is called a Lauhala Basket, handmade by Hawaiian women, but she looked right past me, stifling a yawn. *You have no idea how disinterested I am*, she seemed to say. So I stopped talking. And when she said, "How much you pay?" I pretended not to hear and turned back to my table. I tread carefully when I talk about money with anyone who seems to have plenty of it, even if they bring the subject of money up.

Especially if they bring it up.

This carefulness is even more pronounced now, ever since an old friend from college married a man who made millions in Silicon Valley doing something that has something to do with something I can't recall, fathom, or explain, except that my friend is now something I do understand: ultra-rich. Some years ago, we ordered wine in a restaurant I couldn't afford because she can do whatever she pleases: redecorate, travel, acquire real-estate, *and pay for this dinner?* I hoped. Once the alcohol hit my bloodstream, the what-do-I-*really*-think clock started to tick and, boom, I had to go and question, aloud, a life where money seems to matter more than personal happiness (she *was* unhappy, she made that clear). I mean, honest to Pete, why did I have to go and say that? I didn't hem and haw either, I just blurted it out.

Both of us sat silent for a moment. I saw her hand start to rub her temple like it does when she doesn't know what to do or say. I heard her take a breath. She exhaled. Some harsh words ensued.

Years passed.

Nearly a decade later, she still hasn't forgiven me.

At one point, I considered apologizing for, like, the umpteenth time, but the thought of that conversation brought me face to face with my current face in the mirror who was decidedly against the idea. Which isn't to say she isn't sorry. It's just that I (she, her, *me*) know that somewhere around the third apology, my friend was just not having it. And when the wild rosebud wreath I'd made for her (but never sent, fearing it wasn't expensive enough) exploded in a puff of dust—which, if you ask me, is a *sign*—I was no longer uncertain about the future of our friendship, I was convinced.

I read that you don't get over loss, it just shifts until you wake up one morning and it's not the first thing you think about. Which is what I told my sister the last time we talked on the phone, when one of us usually tears up about something, and this time I do. "It's like listening to my own heartbeat when I hear your voice," I tell her, because it's true. And when the subject of my college friend came up, I said that I was "over it."

I'm not over it.

I'm no longer flooded with regret, but I'm still soggy.

By the time I walk off the ferry, I smell rain and know that tomorrow's ferry ride will likely be spent inside the cabin. But for now, topside, I don't miss a thing about the city and all its troubles that I can never fully understand. And when I think of my college friend who could, at this very moment, be flying with her husband on their private jet to Catalina or Maui, well, my first thought is that I'm sure theirs is not a Learjet. Because they keep *up*.

On a San Juan Island, one can almost believe we are living in an earlier time, those years before highly polarized issues provoke us so regularly we can't figure out what the real issues are fast enough; before forty-year old billionaires bought personal jets *and* personal islands; before too many people bought assault weapons; in a time long before you could read this moments after I write it.

Secrets

August

This story begins with a photo: Pope Francis on the front page of *The New York Times.*

The photo makes me remember a few secrets that need to break loose. When it comes to the Catholic church, there seems to be no end to the secrets that need to break loose.

The Roman Catholic leader is sitting in a wheelchair in a graveyard. Small white crosses surround him. His robes and cap are immaculately white, godly. He traveled to Canada to apologize for the church's role in running boarding schools where Indigenous children were physically and sexually abused and where many died.

Everything about the photo—his carriage, his clasped hands, his air of infallibility—arose in me both gratitude and suspicion. Gratitude because someone influential is doing the right thing, holding himself accountable, asking for forgiveness . . . in the unlikely event that the world is listening. Suspicion because of the infinite number of leaders who speak up *once it is too late.*

It must have occurred to me that many people still care what the Pope has to say about the major issues we face, but when I saw the photo, I realized I hadn't thought about him for so long—if anything, he had become someone I barely remembered being told to care about way back when; it was just what Catholic families did. The Pope was someone we believed in.

When I think back, I didn't *not* believe in him, any more or less than any other presiding man in my life at the time.

One such man comes to mind. A young priest new to our parish. I believed in him right up until he slept with a girl in our high school. I never told my parents what I knew. One Sunday he was gone, a new priest offered Mass, and that was that. Once I left home, I never gave him another thought. *That secret is behind me now.*

But then other secrets began to surface about Catholic priests. Relentless secrets. Who could imagine such things done to children?

They say who we are is rooted in place. But I think who we *become* is rooted in one's need to leave that place. Or stay. And I couldn't wait to leave the steepled white churches and village greens of New England where everything looks serene from the outside, but if there is one thing that predatory priest in high school taught me, it's that deep within, there is shocking chaos.

Here's another secret: One year after the court ruled that Connecticut's anti-abortion law was unconstitutional, my neighborhood friend was pregnant at fifteen. Her father, a successful housing contractor, had abused her for years. He wore an expensive suit to church. That's what my mother called it, "an expensive suit." One day her mother took her into the city. When they came home, my friend was no longer pregnant. I knew this, but we never talked about it. Not in any detail, anyway. Something about everything felt very hidden after that. I didn't know what to do with all the secrets piling on, but they affected me.

There is an image recurrent in religious promotion of a bucolic child, hands folded in prayer, looking up to the sky as if someone up there *knows*. I never saw myself in that face. But I've never called myself an atheist or agnostic, those words rub me the wrong way. *Disheartened* is as close as I come to defining my current relationship to the church. All my life I have defied this idea that any one religion has all the "answers." I could no sooner believe in a one-size-fits-all religion than I could in a short-tempered god peering down at my every move.

But the questions?

Writers are nothing if not open to the questions. I am right now sitting alone on a chaise lounge by a beautiful beach. I came here to swim. But am I swimming? No. I am turning these questions inside out, waiting for something hidden to fall out. *Secrets. Secrets. Secrets.*

I can drive myself a little crazy like this.

But every once in a while I like to reach back to some of the traditions I grew up with. The Catholic stuff I love to avoid is still the Catholic stuff I love to study. To listen to the Pope now may be a way of showing respect to my Catholic past, even if I've mostly lost that respect. Which is why I suddenly need to know what Pope Francis had to say about the recent reversal of Roe v. Wade.

And here it is in black and white, the reason for my suspicion: he strongly opposes all abortions, equating them to "hiring a hitman to solve a problem."

Another Catholic red flag. *Dear Catholic Church: You crush my heart again and again.*

Pope Francis proves that avoidance of hypocrisy is not something we can ever assume from the church, any more than from Congress or the Supreme Court. *And, Francis, see, I wanted to believe in you.*

In the same article I read, "What appears to be something that could never happen again often grows into something grim, but all too real. This isn't progress but a willingness to quickly normalize the extreme."

Heat rose to my cheeks.

Catholics (Catholic *girls*) are raised to not mention the white elephant in the room, to say nothing even though we can clearly see what is what. And who is what. And who is getting away with what. The church tried to drum fear of the elephant into us and curiosity out of us. *Shhh, now, hush, hush. Be quiet. It's a secret.*

Those teachings didn't exactly stick. And I think it's time to give myself a round of applause (a standing ovation!) for seeing through all the scheming duplicities, even as a kid. There should be a huge grant for kids who survive masses of religious pretense and hypocrisy and go on to become writers.

I'd apply.

Back on June twenty-fourth, my neighbor cheered on her lanai when Roe v. Wade was reversed. She had friends in to celebrate. One man arrived waving a tiny American flag. He looked harmless enough, so I asked him what the party was about, knowing full well. I noticed he was charged with a fervent energy I have come to recognize in people who don't mind saying yes to guns but no to abortion. It's a look that takes over not only his eyes, but his whole expression. He grins but it's a harsh grin. His nose flairs. His claws sharpen. "We are living in a pro-life country now," he said.

"Really? Pro-life?" I said, prepared by all the reading I'd done on the issue, hoping to find some sign that the vote might be overturned, or at least challenged. And let me tell you, as I spoke I cared nothing about what anyone thought about me and everything about what I know is true and right. "Because you don't seem to mind what happens to the baby after it is born. Let me get this straight, how does one say no to abortion, but it's okay that there hasn't been a single week in 2022 without a mass shooting? By the way, you are only stopping *safe* abortions. Women, likely the poorest women, will die."

By then two other men had arrived at my neighbor's door. I thought, *Taliban*.

I've read that writers should never explain, only portray, but I can't help but want to explain that it wasn't fear that made me speak up. Nor pride, nor any need to "win."

No. It was the simple effect of skilled, hands-on, pressure.

Earlier that day, scared for the future of reproductive choice, I'd booked a massage to calm me. The therapist kept saying, "Oh! I need to unblock you. You are so tight." And then she'd press down on just the right spot and say, "There, can you feel it?"

And to my surprise, I could. Little pops. Especially in my neck, where a firm spine meets an ever churning mind. *Knots of worry. Knots of fear. Pop. Pop. Pop.* And then a sort of flooding sensation, as if something gave way, and an honest-to-god peacefulness came over me. I forced myself not to doubt the feeling. To *believe*.

Before beginning my massage, the therapist had agreed that it was a sad day for women. When it was over, I sat up and admitted my secret to her, one that I'd been holding onto since the age of nineteen. I didn't feel ready to share this secret aloud. But I felt ready to *be* ready.

Actually, it's hard to capture just how ready I felt.

Instead of lapsing into embarrassed silence, the therapist leaned in so that her brow briefly met mine and then a small miracle happened; she admitted *her* secret to me, one that she'd been holding onto since the age of sixteen. Our secrets were no longer hidden under anything, but spread through the air. We opened to a truth of ourselves, and in that lavender scented room, we had a private opportunity to share exactly what that truth was. I was her. She was me. And we were millions of other women.

My experience with massages, actually the whole way I feel about the neuromuscular system, had changed in an hour. Not only had my physical and mental stress been unlocked, but the door to the shame closet flew open, and another secret took wing. All the freer for having been kept too long.

After the story broke about the ten-year-old Ohio girl who was raped and then had to flee her state in order to have a safe and legal abortion, I booked another massage, but not with the same therapist. I wanted to set apart what felt like one of the most honest encounters of my life.

I believe it always will.

A Good Day In Our Inner City

September

O n a warm evening in early September, a friend came over to watch a movie. What we *really* wanted was to indulge in popcorn drenched in butter and enough salt and brewer's yeast to make it a luscious breather from real life.

It is so good to get a breather from real life.

She and I have been friends for ages—despite a few bumps in the road during the Trump administration. So when she suggested that, instead of a movie, I stop resisting and finally watch the KOMO News Documentary, *Seattle is Dying,* I couldn't decide whether to object or make myself a Negroni and give in.

I know. *You* saw it ages ago.

Everyone saw it ages ago.

But me? I didn't want to watch it. I grew fretful just thinking about watching it. When it first came out in 2019, I was living in my own little dying neighborhood, already fearful about walking anywhere at night. By 2021, even in daylight, so much about downtown Seattle was dangerously scary. When she first suggested we watch the documentary back in the summer of 2020, I suggested that we reschedule to a day when I hadn't seen anyone shooting up in a stairwell. She wanted to watch it anyway. I suggested an episode of Call the Midwife.

But to have a friend, we must be one.

So, well, fine. I agreed to watch.

But first I wanted to look up who owns KOMO News. "Hmmm," I said slowly, wilting into the couch. The right-biased Sinclair News Group. Nothing ruins good popcorn faster than bad news, I thought, thinking I'd react to the documentary in the same way I've come to view cable news—that we are not being told the truth, that preaching to our own choir is not trustworthy reporting, it is mostly for entertainment purposes, and it is divisive.

The thing is, I was riveted. There wasn't anything the commentator said that I hadn't thought of myself. I wanted to stop watching but I couldn't. At one point I had to fan myself with a throw pillow.

Generally, I back away even from the words "right" and "left," let alone the idea of edging my way closer to the side of KOMO on the issues of homelessness and addiction. Yet, that edging felt more like barreling as the documentary continued.

"Seattle never looks like this in the real estate magazines," my friend said.

Right up until the day we moved out of Belltown, all things considered, I thought I was doing a pretty good job of coping, because the thought of moving, of upheaving my whole life, makes me a little crazy. Plus, I was in the middle of a book project, already seriously challenged by the many cooks in the many kitchens of publishing.

But lately I'm trying to give more thought to accepting how things are and moving on if something or someone causes me pain, forgiving the perpetrator, as well as myself, along the way.

I am even trying to forgive Seattle's city council for—well, you know—all of it.

Though I may be holding on to a little grudge. It's so hard to forgive stubborn incompetence, and too many council members are appallingly lacking in leadership skills.

But I'm not going to give up on our city. I didn't give up on New York in the early nineties or after 9/11. And today, I feel safer when I return to Manhattan than I do on the downtown streets of Seattle. Last time I visited Washington Square Park, I thanked a mounted policeman for being there. When he asked me where I lived and I told him, he said, "Oh, I'd never work in that city. People love us here." That may or may not be true, but as he tipped his hat to the couple walking by, I was moved by how people seemed to welcome his presence.

In Seattle's downtown, the decline may be quieter than a plane destroying a city's two largest towers, but even so, it is never discreet.

But before Covid?

It was loud. Literally, *booming*. When everything old was torn down so that everything new could be built, when the Amazon campus was going up and up along with the condos and skyscrapers we called by name quicker than I would have ever thought—Insignia, Spire, The Emerald—technology wealth was new to the city and so was I. My husband and I moved into a building on Fifth and Vine. We lived on the fifth floor with a view of the Space Needle.

Today, it's hard to believe that in 2017, CNN named Belltown the best place to live in the Seattle metro area, calling it "a walkable neighborhood with everything you need." As I remember it, "everything" mostly meant happy hours. And let me just say, there were some pretty great happy hours. One night I had a book release party that grew raucous with laughter and dance music. My neighbor (I should have invited him to avoid his complaint) called the police. And like *that*, they arrived.

Those were the days.

How quickly an urban neighborhood can change.

But honestly, I was ready for a change even before Covid made living in Belltown intolerable for me. My friend Stephanie still lives in my old building. She loves Seattle, and regrets its decline as much as I do. "I'm not going to leave," she said. "This is my home and I'm going to see this through." I worry about her, though, because every time we talk, she shares another horror story—the addict who snuck in and left blood and feces all over the walls of her workplace bathroom; the man who set fire to the restaurant across the street for no apparent reason (she has footage of him crumbling newspaper, layering it along the foundation, striking a match, people walking by); and the shootings, the constant, seemingly random, shootings.

But a part of me is glad that she is staying. For one thing, I'm hoping the good people who stay will balance out the ruthless fentanyl dealers. Even if hoping for something rarely makes it so. Even if I met another woman on the bus who said she would never go downtown. Even if this seems like the greatest threat to our city, this fear of what downtown has become. And for another, Seattle can't keep on this way. That last string of shootings—six fatalities in one night—has got to be Seattle hitting bottom. Right?

But some of our stories still highlight the best of our city. This is when our tone moves from frustration to that of allies, as though we can't help but speak fondly of a city that the media declares is "dying."

People are desperate for normalcy, and more than anything, "normalcy" in Seattle means a walk by the waterfront. When I walk down Alaskan Way and see a flowing stream of tourists enchanted by the view that is sort of the whole point of walking downtown, I remember how taken I was the first time I saw Puget Sound. Everywhere I look, there is enjoyment. I think, *This is going to be one hell of a city again when they figure things out.*

I keep watching.

One woman takes her partner's hand. I find a renewed sense of hope in their awe and in their smiles, which, for me, counts as a really good moment in our inner city nowadays.

The Italian Festival

October

My good acquaintance Dennis invited me to sign copies of my latest title at Seattle's Italian Festa.

I was thrilled. The invitation gets better: "I can't find another Italian author this year. People are still hesitant about crowds. You can have the table to yourself."

An invitation like this doesn't come along all that often, and not because I don't *want* to sign copies at cultural festivals. It's that booth fees are generally too high. There is no way it would be a cost-effective venture for someone selling books.

Now, at a festival celebrating all things Italian—and by "all things" I mean what 99 percent of the people come for: the food—if I were selling gelato like the booth to my immediate right, or cannoli like the booth to my immediate left (making it pleasantly clear that this was not a book fair where table placement is determined by pecking order), well then, yes, I could afford the booth fee. I could afford the moon.

Here in the Northwest, a late-September open-air festival is so needed because everyone knows the warm weather will go by fast, faster still because we haven't even *been* to a festival in two years—years when I would read the news and have to stop; when I would hear the news on the radio and have to turn it off.

So of course I accepted the invitation.

Then I proceeded to ask (wish, long) for a fee I could afford, because sometimes you just have to swallow your pride, stop tiptoeing around the truth, and ask. Even if your chances are slim, it's good to try. There are boring after-effects for playing it safe.

I figured the next best thing for me to do would be to show up and be willing to graciously navigate how to interact in the current state of covid-fear. Fear-levels are poles apart lately, and it's too easy to say the wrong thing and make a big mistake about people's fears. Huge, gigantic, massive mistakes. I don't even try to make sense of it anymore.

But first things first. I had to create enough of a display to turn my assigned space into a genuine "booth" and not just another book-signing-table-top. For days, booth-design was just about all I cared about. Time would tell if I'd come up with an inviting exhibition. In the meantime, I bought a new lipstick in a deep (but not too) shade of red. I knew my booth needed something more. And lipstick is cheap.

My first no-sale of the day was a man who picked up my latest book and read the cover. I tried to summarize what the book is about, which is really hard to do. It's like asking someone to explain, briefly, who they are. He nodded, but I could tell from his eyes that I'd lost him.

You do tend to lose people going on about your book.

The key is finding balance between explanation and too much. You want to say enough to make the book appealing but leave room for imagination. All while live music was playing so loud that I had to shout to be heard while struggling not to dance because when I hear good music, I can't help myself. Finally, I had to stop bonding with the music and the food. In the beginning I tried to do it all. But a couple of no-sales later, I had to decide: Do I want to eat and dance the weekend away, or do I want to sell books?

The man turned my book over to read the back. He read the cover again. He read the *spine*. He lowered his mask and took about twenty minutes telling me about his own writing. He told me about his grown children he never sees. He told me about his red necktie. He was talking only to talk, but this is normal. The world is full of lonely people. If I even begin to imagine how many, I could cry. Finally, I say, "Is it possible that you really want to buy yourself a new book you seem interested in?"

It was not.

He set the book down and walked away shaking his head. But not in just an I-don't-like-your-book way. It was more like the sort of head shake that might be given to the rest of the population by, say, a ruling colonizer. Still, in some mysterious way, I did think that my book had affected him somehow. In the end, I thought the whole encounter was funny. Just not laugh-out-loud-ha-ha-ha-ha-ha funny.

My poise was a little ruffled, as you can imagine.

And in my stomach, a heaviness. Like a wet bag of sand. Just this weight. I had hours and hours and hours to go. And a wish that I could wave a wand, this once, and make the whole weekend pass quickly.

And then.

A teacher looked through my new children's book and said, "I'll take five of these."

Oh, those words.

Those generous words.

Things were looking up. My confidence soared. I don't at all question the effect of confidence. Time and again it has proved that it can return out of the blue, dressed just like my sister-in-law (also a teacher who loves palazzo pants). *I can't help it*, I thought, *I love this. I love selling my books!* You'd think I'd love the whole wide world of internet connection, but for me, the best experience is all about meeting my readers.

Suddenly everything seemed possible. Even a profit.

I smiled. I smiled so hard I started to laugh.

L ord knows, I've been selling my creativity my entire life.

I know you must be thinking, really, your *entire* life? But I have. Since year five I've been honing my skills: Hand painted rocks. Lemonade with a touch of anise. Popsicles with pansies frozen within, edible art long before its time. Handmade puppets, clutches, notecards. Drumming up business. Scared to death, but excited. *Alive.*

A woman walked by my booth with a little dog in a harness on one leash and a little girl in a harness on another. I never thought I'd see the day.

The dog yipped and yipped.

The little girl whined.

The woman had long red hair and wore an elegant black dress draped with a bold purple shawl tied at the waist that made her look at once stylish and clashing. She seemed to have arrived from Paris, possibly by way of Fremont. She walked right by my booth without so much as a glance, and for all the reasons I think it's wrong to harness a toddler, I was relieved.

Next, a well-dressed man (white shirt, tie, leather shoes, dress pants made of whatever it is that fabric with a sheen is made of these days; a fit physique that made me think, *perfetto,* though part of his hair was possibly not his own) chided me a little when I couldn't answer his question in Italian. I often feel like I am too Italian compared to the general population in this city. But today, he is not the first person who has made me feel like I am not Italian *enough.* I sighed and thought, *What he thinks, he will think, whether I worry about it or not.*

Which is how I feel about a lot of my relatives back East.

And why I moved West.

Two men slowed down to stare at my table. "Wait," one said, "I know your name. I love your column." I felt like I could coast on that kudo for the rest of the day. Then they looked at each other. They stared. They sized each other up. "Do we know each other?" the younger of the two said. And from the other, "I think we maybe did . . . once. Only once." It was clear they didn't know what more to say.

We never really know what to say a lot of the time, do we?

Suddenly, I was standing in a place so unlike my office where stories are written and, instead, where they are made. Finally, the younger one laughed—I've always been an admirer of anyone who can save the day with laughter—and the older man bought two books, one for himself and one "for my friend here," in what seemed like a real gesture of delight.

Still coasting on the confidence that makes for easier *every*thing, I was reminded that festivals are about getting out of the pitiful small world of our phone, our laptop, our *head*. They are about meeting people (or re-meeting them), where no one is really focused on one part of the festival but making their way through it all, our genuine social lives returned to us under a remarkably clear, deep blue sky.

Hard to think it was the same sky that pours down so much rain today. But I spend more hours writing when it rains, more time recalling things . . . like when a festival teaches me about people. And patience. And the next one I manage to plead my way into, I hope to learn more.

On Sunday, I was out of books (out of books!), so I packed up my booth a little early, and on my way out the door, I turned back to see Dennis leaning against a wall, watching the band play the kind of feel-good music that gets people up to dance, and then they keep right on dancing. I stood there for a while thinking how Dennis had just pulled off Seattle's thirtieth Italian festival with knack and finesse, and he was still smiling.

Though I sensed that a change had come over him, relief had entered his emotions, likely. And I know enough about pulling off an event to know how relief can sometimes feel deflating.

I wished I could have stayed and danced, but I had to go, and I didn't want to bother Dennis with one more thing, not even a personal "ciao e grazie di tutto" which can take a lot of oomph, good oomph for its recipient, but still *oomph*.

So, I'm saying it here.

Crazy

December

My Aunt Connie used to sit me down at the kitchen table to share tales of her great journey from Abruzzo to New York. About how young and scared she was, but also how hopeful. A month after arriving, she went to work for the Department of Public Service and stayed there until her retirement. A rock in our family, we could always count on her. If one of us needed help, she'd cook up some pasta and *listen*. Everything will work out, she'd say, *tutto funzionerà*.

Today, her story stays with me: On her first day of work, when people asked her where she was from, she was afraid to say. But afraid as she was to admit she was from a country that had sided with Germany in "la guerra" (and then she would cross herself), she was never uncertain of how to answer. She was nothing *but* sure. Until her death, she lived in exactly two places: the war-torn village she left behind, and in what she referred to as "dis (meaning *this*) country." But beyond a sincere appreciation for "dis country," she never really thought of it as *casa*. Home.

On the opposite side of this country, people move to Seattle from all over the world, drawn to its natural beauty, work opportunities, independence, and openness. Since my earliest days of writing about this city, there have been so many new arrivals that Seattle—or the perception of it—has begun to feel more like an opinion, heightened in our minds by background, political leaning, and personal experience. And many of our conversations also begin with the question, "Where are you from?"

But it's always the same reluctance on my part. Unlike my favorite aunt, I can still be so *un*sure.

Am I from New England, the place of my formative years, where I went to college, and why New York will always feel like "my" city? Or am I from the Northwest because I've lived here longer? A huge part of me still feels like I'm from the Olympic Peninsula where I was first married and owned my first home, my first dance studio, and where a sense of place returns whenever I talk to friends there. While another part belongs to Seattle, home to me for the better part of two decades after I grew weary of living in a small, isolated town. Still, another part is from Oahu, the island where my mother's ashes lie; where I return whenever work slows down enough to let me be with her again. To save time, as well as emotional toll, whenever I'm on the island and a sunburned tourist asks, "Do you live here?" I don't hesitate. I say, "Yes." Today, the most adaptable part of me is from Bainbridge Island, because by 2021, Seattle became too demoralizing for many of us who lived downtown.

And much of me feels as if I am from Southern Italy, where my DNA derives more of a sense of belonging than anywhere else, even though I've visited only twice. On both those trips, I felt as if I could relax into exactly who I am. I was meant to live in this country, I thought during one smog-pink sunset in Sorrento, the sapphire waters of the Gulf of Naples beneath the balcony of our *pensione*. That thought repeated itself over and over as the unhurried weeks passed by.

Honestly, I can still have such strong sensations of displacement that when my sister called from her new home in Florida to tell me about the snakes and alligators that, after Hurricane Ian, hid from view in the puddles after being flooded out of their ponds and burrows, an intense wave of empathy came over me. I kept imagining myself peeping out from under the murky, oil-slicked pools, clinging to the bottom with my toes, moving my hips back and forth to keep from cramping. Does this make me a truly compassionate person or just one with a crazy imagination?

I don't know anymore.

When I tell this story to my friend in New York, also a writer and also Italian, she laughs. As with most conversations, especially between two writers, we move on to discuss our current projects at length. Writing might not offer the same challenges as scaling the side of a mountain or climbing slippery rock, but when we talk about the ups and downs, those are exactly the metaphors we use. Finally, I ask her what she would call this sense of home-uncertainty I keep trying to describe. "Well," she says, and then she falls silent for a moment. I want to urge her on, but you don't want to interrupt a writer when she is this quiet. "I don't know what *they* (meaning anyone not living in New York) would call it, but I (meaning all Italians or all Italians living in New York, I'm not sure) think writers and crazy are pretty much the same thing."

I think it occurred to us at the same moment that we actually liked the sound of this. For a second I thought about objecting to say that the word "crazy" isn't the same as "crazy imagination." That "crazy" is not really okay with me.

Except that it is.

And I don't feel any sense of alarm about this. I could bemoan the truth and drive myself even crazier, or I could accept it; wrap my mind around the fact that this is one of those qualities over which I have no say whatsoever.

Which makes me re-remember my Aunt Connie. Who was, and still is, an honest-to-goodness saint in my life, the largest imaginable kind, the size of my every hope (past, present, and future), desire, and purpose.

Actually, I don't think I can measure the size of her effect on me. It would be like trying to measure just how successful I've been in life. But for some reason, I don't feel like taking any account of that just yet.

So, as often happens at the end of my writing day, the beginning of my story, *voilà*, becomes the perfect close: *tutto funzionerà.*

2023

Lists, A Revelation, and A Whole Other Story

January

This is the first time in nearly a month that I've sat down to write anything but a list.

I don't keep lists on my phone. I like to write them out. All through December, there was a list on my laptop, one in the kitchen that had to remember to find its way into my bag before I left the house, and one that was never allowed to leave my bag in the first place.

I'm not exactly sure *why* lists calm me the way they do.

It takes me about two minutes to figure this out.

When I was a kid, December grew into The Enemy I Could Not See. My mother turned into a tenser version of herself, and that is putting it mildly. Her expectations, frustration, and disappointments override my earliest December memories.

But who could blame her?

Who wouldn't be tense if it is assumed that you alone will need to satisfy the holiday expectations of so many others?

Years later, I asked her why she put so much pressure on herself—frankly, on all of us—to have the "perfect" Christmas. "What do you mean, I love Christmas," she said, as though she couldn't stand to have her daughter recall her as she really was.

And it was a feat, pulling off the magic for three kids who watched TV commercials, a husband who never lifted a finger inside the house, and a disapproving mother and competitive sister who judged her traditional feasts so critically. I began to grasp just enough about guilt to see that I did not know exactly why my mother *had* to live up to so many expectations, only that she must.

Maybe I sensed it was setting a precedent I couldn't see myself upholding. Which turned out to be true. I've never known a mother's level of holiday stress, but I can see now why I am always a little annoyed at the holiday, a little untrusting of its motives, and why my mood begins to dig a little trench around it as soon as I hear the first carol, which comes earlier and earlier every year so that by the twenty-fifth of December, it's more of a moat.

So I began last month pretty much how I always begin December, by telling myself that I am too busy to entertain. I was still shaking off the effects of a Thanksgiving setback when I had to relearn that I should never drink Prosecco with my guests while the fowl is still in the oven. Not unless I have a backup plan. And backup plans aren't generally as festive. Or as satisfying.

I tried. I really did.

Nevertheless, by Christmas Eve, I was at it again. The scent of basil, garlic, and tomatoes filled the air of my home, nothing higher-on-the-food-chain than pasta this time, the food that plants me firmly to this earth, served in my heirloom ceramic pasta bowl that always adds festivity to our table.

But it's more than that, my mother was happiest in the kitchen when not under pressure, she loved to cook. And I loved seeing how relaxed she became when she was just being herself.

Still, I'm no cook, it's not my mother's kitchen over here, believe me. People don't come to my table to ooh and aah over the food. They ooh and ahh over the fact that I have made the food. And so do I.

I think what happened was once the lights were strung all over town, the golden hue that says, "It's December, have some fun, your desk will still be there in January," the brightness allowed the best part of the season to come to light: eating and laughing with people I enjoy. Low stress. High spirits.

And, sadly, on one occasion, the opposite of high spirits.

It was just something that happens between people, a sudden something, something unpleasant, defeating the purpose of coming together. I know this person has issues with dissatisfaction and control (honestly, she is the most controlling person I have ever met), but it took her insulting my clothes, a skirt I love so much I bought *two*, to push me to the end. When she pronounced my skirt "inappropriate," I doubt she stopped to consider that I was also disapproving of her, of her judginess, her tactlessness.

But I'm not unsympathetic. I know that judgy, tactless behavior is often a vent for insecurity. Even so, there are some people you just need to prune back in the new year. Maybe it's that simple.

Except it's never that simple. Pruning takes a toll.

I said nothing so she wouldn't know how stung I was. (Fortunately, I'm much better at silence. 2022 was a milestone year for me in this regard.)

But once I was home, I cried. First to my husband. Then to my sister, who is like my insides when it comes to matters of sensitivities. But here is the clincher: I thought my tears were all about what was said about my skirt. Only later could I see that I may have cried more about my own deep-seated fear: when I bought the skirts, I was five years younger.

Am I suffering the results of my own denial? This is the question I repeated over and over to myself for days. Until I finally raised my hand and said, *maybe so, okay, yes.*

It's a writer's dream to dig in deep like this and not come up empty handed, so the *idea* of exposing this revelation feels great.

The reality is embarrassing.

So that's it.

That's what happened.

As I was saying.

I began my December-shift-of-attitude by pre-washing the wine glasses and hand-painted plates from Italy, dishes I found at an estate sale, the whole set for thirty bucks on a day when I was feeling unsettled because we'd just moved to a new home. Oddly, standing in front of a departed woman's dishes, I came to life. Those dishes put images in my head of a housewarming party happening distinctly in my kitchen; of saying goodbye to my old neighborhood, and hello to new possibilities.

Beautiful dishes do cast a spell over me, so I slid my arm around my husband's back and said, "We are buying these dishes." And he, being him, said, "We don't *need* more dishes, do we?" So I looked at him with my *I'm not kidding* eyes and he bent over to pick up the box.

Now, one of the best parts of writing a list is being able to cross things off. There, done, *finito*. Next? As a result, there were a lot of trips to the market in December.

On one, I stood in line behind a woman wearing six inch heels, and though I've never known what it's like to feel *that* elevated, it stirred another memory of my mother in kitten heel slingbacks clicking down the aisles of the Stop & Shop, *click, click, click,* a look of mastery coming over her, pure focus in her eyes. There was clicking in my head, my stomach, running through my arms and legs, reminding me that our muscles are cells of memory. They build around our stories and won't let go.

On another trip to Town & Country (T & C to the locals), once I left the store, I needed to repack the weight in my bags, so I set my groceries out on a table.

Watching me from the next table was a family from India: a young man who spoke good English with a Mumbaikar accent, nothing short of melodious. His father also spoke English but not as well, and his mother and grandmother (facial lines etched deep) didn't speak English at all. I gathered the three older adults were visiting their Amazon-employed son/grandson. The men talked about "the Dow being down three points," or maybe they said three hundred. I have never understood a thing about what this means. But the women kept nodding at me.

I smiled at them. They smiled at me.

Who was it that said they were old enough to be "in the years of unselfconsciousness?" No longer able to contain themselves, they rushed over to help me repack my groceries. Or not to help, exactly, but to inspect my food. You would have thought I was unpacking pounds of gold. Both wore colorful saris under their coats, one bright purple, the other green, which I loved. So few women bother to wear anything but leggings nowadays, so the saris touched me, gave me a lift. As did the semicircles of turmeric under the older woman's nails as she admired my heirloom tomato, reaching into my bag to pull out another.

Food is what these women could relate to in this strange, new country where many of us are too reserved or phone-distracted to give into childlike curiosity. I find it moving when someone is so interested and present; so wholeheartedly *there*.

Just as the younger woman picked up my box of lasagna noodles, her son came running up to scold her, too harshly, I thought. What's the right way to say this—it's fine to be embarrassed by your mother, who hasn't been? But to yell at her in public as if she is a misbehaved child is not okay. But here's what is true about so many cultures the world over: boys can do no wrong. She took the scolding with eyes that said, "To the world you are my son, but to me you *are* the world. No matter what you say. No matter what you do."

If the women are here to stay, it may take years for them to find a true sense of belonging. Culturally, it's a tough task of what to give up and what to keep. But we always keep our food. Food *is* culture.

I have no proof of any of this of course, other than I know longing for connection when I see it. And I recognize two women in search of something of which they are not exactly sure. Just witnessing how excited my food made them kindled some of my deepest recognitions, ones learned by heart, possibly before I was born. (Here is where I hear my poet friend Kevin say, "Don't use the word *heart*. Women always do this." But, Kevin, I ask you, what is wrong with the word? Its meaning is clear, and it helps us feel optimistic. If we let go of the word and everything it implies, what will we replace it with?)

I wanted to talk to the women, and I did for a while, the son translating my questions. (I was right about Mumbai/ Amazon/their son/their relocating), and when he asked, "Do you have children?" and I said "no," they looked so sad for me.

They always do.

And it's hard to say, "No, wait, I chose my life," to people who haven't had the benefit of living so freely. My mind ran through a few of the things they could be thinking: *That is not imaginable in our culture. What about family? It is not proper for a woman to be out in the world alone.*

I excused myself, wished them well. I still had to walk home and make dinner. A friend was coming over.

When I opened the door, I smiled to myself. My friend wore black leggings under a long gray duster sweater. The height of chic in the Pacific Northwest.

I took her by the hand, and we started to talk.

The Walk

February

Once a month I walk with a small group of women. We meet for company and exercise, of course, but we also like to blow off steam about the state of the world, so there is always much to talk about.

Unspoken rule number one is that we air personal matters first. I can't speak for the others, but there are times when I don't really know what to think, what to feel, what I want to think or want to feel, or even what to believe until I say what's on my mind. So for me, these walks are like coming up for air. I believe in the therapeutic effect of sharing our plights with people we trust. It's the best help out there, as far as I'm concerned.

Without these talks, without a doubt, life would be harder.

First up today, one of us (we all have names, but I promised) talks about how hard it's been to make decisions about her aging parents' care. "I know this is all part of life," she says in a way that sounds as if she's said it a lot lately, like a coping chant, and I can see the dark circles under her eyes where all the decisions have gathered to keep her from sleeping. She turns away to give herself a chance to collect herself and we stand quietly for a moment, wondering what more we might do to help her get past the worst of it; knowing these kinds of choices won't get easier as time moves on. I give her a hug from the side to remind her that we've all been in her shoes or will be soon. To brighten the mood, I say, "Everyday, I'm going to do what I love. I'm going to write and dance and bike and swim. Even if the chlorine and salt are ruining my hair."

"It's just hair," our oldest walker says. Hair does not, in her view, bear too much examination.

After that, we start in on the news, and believe me, we have as much to say about the Bryan Kohbergers of the world as we do the Putins. But that's not the point. The point is, once we hit the news front, our concerns feel even more pressing. Which leads to us walking a little closer together.

"I have to figure out how to sleep again," one of us says as she stops to watch two crows, "and if I do fall asleep, I startle myself awake." One crow stretches out its neck, inviting the other to preen its feathers, and we all pause to take in the display. Birds have never let her down and never will, she told us once. At the time, she was "celebrating" her divorce, that's how she put it, and her tone was light that afternoon when she said she wouldn't mind finding someone, someday, but for now she just wants to be *aloooone*, drawing out the word as much as its meaning. "I mean, I'd like to have a better relationship with a man before I'm done for, as long as he's self-supporting, has a sense of humor, and isn't a jerk," she drew in a breath, "even though it's my personal belief that he doesn't exist."

Her tone, though, is *not* light today.

Her tone is not light because her daughter goes to Washington State University in Pullman where the man charged with the Moscow, Idaho stabbings was a graduate student. And now she has this underlying fear for her daughter in a way she never had before. "I try not to stress," she says, "by working a lot, staying busy. Shopping online, that's the worst escape." She pauses. "Or the best." And though you can tell she doesn't want to look as if she's enjoyed her own joke too much, she can't help it, she laughs. And we laugh, too.

But no one tries to find consolation or meaning in anything that occurred that early morning in Idaho. We know when it's best to just let one of us hate something about the world when we need to, and that sometimes we just can't make things better, safer, easier, than they really are. I've often wondered what it must be like to live in Pullman or Moscow these days, to deal with a tragedy that is so much more menacing than the average small-town crisis. I think how important these walks are because you can't ease your fearfulness with your own fearfulness. You can't do it alone. Our skin is not as thick as we want to believe.

The weight of the stabbings in Moscow continues to wash over us, removing any desire I have to bring up the story that made me say aloud to a complete stranger sitting next to me on the ferry, "I can't believe this!" Which made her look at my *New York Times* and say, "Oh, god, what now?"

The headline read: Six-*Year-Old Shoots Teacher At Virginia Elementary School.*

Before leaving the house to come on this walk, I did a little homework to add to the conversation I had intended to bring up: how nine states have now instituted an assault weapons ban. Which is so important because (is what I would have said) the Highland Park shooter was able to buy multiple assault weapons, despite two incidents in 2019 in which he threatened to kill himself and his family. I was also going to share a quote I read in *The Seattle Times:* "In Seattle alone, the data shows violent crime rising so fast that thirty years of progress may be undone in a blink." And I'm sure the fact that there were thirty-eight mass shootings in the first twenty-one days of this new year would have come up, how much it disturbs us that this is where we are in America 2023.

As for what to believe . . . I don't know if all the shootings are because we have such a long history of owning guns in this country as well as manufacturing them, or that we've grown desensitized to the misery and havoc they wreak, or that there is such a stigma about mental health issues, and too little money appropriated for mental health support, or the violent video games played by so many boys so that eventually they may want to try the real thing, or all the websites and chat rooms full of misinformation, or the mainstream news that tends to simplify the issues for mass consumption—including the ramifications of gun violence on our psyches—or that we as a people refuse to admit that things have gone so terribly wrong, or some combination of any or all of the above. But if I think too long and too hard about any one of these reasons, I sink right down into despair.

Abyss is the word that comes to mind.

And I don't want to bring the others down with me, not now, not today, for another reason too: one of us invited a friend to join us today, a woman I know . . . well, tried to know and decided, *no*. Though for years, without knowing why, I was drawn to her.

I don't remember which horrible school shooting had just occurred, pick one, when she and I sat next to each other at Eleven Winery one Sunday afternoon, and against my better judgment, when she brought up the subject of gun control, I was honest.

Quite soon after, so was she.

So I learned that she is not exactly pro-gun so much as she is anti-take-our-guns-away, and she is passionately opinionated about gun rights. I'm passionately opinionated, too, so that's not why I don't want to bring up the story. I don't want to bring it up with someone, anyone, who just might say what she said that day in a winery shining with sun, when anger rose in my throat and I left thinking, *How can someone still think—say—there is no connection between the number of guns out there, so easily obtained, and the number of children who have been killed because of them? Guns don't lie. Facts about guns don't lie. People lie. To themselves. To the world.*

I wonder if she saved the photo she took of us that day where I'm leaning toward her, though I could tell by my smile that I was trying too hard. It's awkward—and nearly impossible for me—to be open and honest while also holding back, afraid to say too much about myself, my work, my likes and dislikes, because I am slowly realizing that the person I am talking to is not someone I fully trust.

Now, wait, yes, I get that there is room for all sides of an issue, or most issues. And, yes, I'm as tired of the *us* versus *them* mindset as the next person. And, yes, yes, we should listen to and respect opposing viewpoints, it's the only way to heal division, to mend what is broken.

But on *this* issue, when I think of all the children who have been shot at school (at school!), I'm afraid I can't make room for all the guns and all the people who say we should own as many of them as we like. I know—have known since the Amish School Shooting—that on this matter I draw the line. I can't listen to anything more about guns from the point of view of a gun-rights advocate. I can't hear anything more about guns from the eyes of someone who chooses guns over children.

Nor does any part of me want to repeat the mistake I made when I insulted a colleague about this issue, but I don't trust myself not to. It wasn't *every*thing I said, it was only the last word—not even a word, really, a mere syllable—that made her hang up: "Take away the gun and all you have is another lonely, angry person who needs help, but without the ability to kill so many people so fast! *Duh*."

I went too far, I know this, but it's too late.

So, today we will just have to leave our talk with a knife.

In Moscow. That hasn't been found. Yet. And leave guns for another time.

Which doesn't mean my mind hasn't been forming these lines as I walk because one way I manage stress is to write about what causes it.

I don't know why I need to say this.

Well, yes I do.

I say it because writing is really about finding out something more about ourselves and others, and there is always something more. Like when our quietest walker who usually looks at the bright side and never, ever swears, throws her head back and yells, "If I hear one more person talk about their fucking thoughts and prayers!" after the deadly shooting in Virginia at Walmart, I think it was, but again, pick one. And then she said what we were all thinking, "Those words have come to mean exactly what they will achieve, not a goddamn thing."

A teenager walks by absorbed in her phone, prompting our oldest walker to speak again, "Has she even looked up at the Olympics? Has she looked at the sky?" More than once we've discussed phone walkers because we are worried that future generations won't look after the natural world if they no longer take the time to be stirred by it, even on a walk.

As if the girl can hear us, she looks up at the scenery. It captures her attention for, like, a millisecond, then eyes right back down.

"Write about that," our friend says.

So I did.

The Bathers

March

You know those mornings when you say to yourself, "I need to do something else today." When you feel tired, stuck, unable to face your inbox; a feeling that causes your chest to tighten even now as you read this.

Not that there haven't been about a million times you've felt like this before, but this time it's like your whole body cries out, *change in routine, please!*

And you think, *I should heed this cry.*

So you jump in the car and head up to the Olympus Spa in Lynnwood and try not to feel guilty about booking the Tropical Korean Moisturizing Service on top of the hot tub soak and body scrub even though it will now cost about as much as flying to Hawaii. Perhaps this is why there is an old Korean proverb that says, "All of one's physical illnesses come from one's mind," which I take as gospel because, luckily, it does not say that they come from Visa.

If you've never heard of a Korean bathing spa, the intense cleansing process called "seshin" involves soaking the body in hot water, then rubbing it with a loofah to thoroughly rid the body of all the dead skin that builds up. (Note: you do not want to look at the floor right after they rinse you. Except that you will. And you will not be able to comprehend how all that gunk came from *you*.)

Here is what I read: Until the 1980s, most Korean households didn't have personal showers at home. The upper classes had personal bathtubs, but the masses went to the rivers or public baths and bathing was considered a means to cure disease. It was also considered a means to cure "the unhappiness that is felt by someone because they do not have anyone to talk to."

Soaking in a huge hot tub with other women whose faces were drowsy and glazed, trying to leave god knows what stresses behind, relaxed me in a way that must have been inside of me somewhere, I just had to find it again, not give up on it. I felt the tightness in my shoulders ease even before the loofah scrub. Or the moisturizing treatment. And, oh why not, the added oily massage.

Today, I am an ocean away from that spa, invited to sign copies of my children's book about dance at a Honolulu production choreographed by a friend of mine. And on my ride in from the airport, what do I see in a small building behind the Convention Center? A huge sign for the Aloha Sauna & Spa. When I ask my Uber driver about it, she says, "When you go holo holo around Waikiki, you go there. Korean ladies will buff you soft as a keiki's bum."

I had just endured a six hour flight in a middle seat next to a snoring man. After googling the meaning of holo

holo, I immediately called the spa. I was just holding my breath to see if they could squeeze me in.

This island is much closer to Korea than the mainland, so most of the women in the spa are new to Hawaii and don't speak English, but that doesn't stop communication, far from it. We don't need words to complete the art of give-and-take. Sound is enough.

But, oh, pardon me for thinking if you've seen one Korean bathing spa that somehow you've seen them all. The scene inside is right out of an eighteenth century painting. "The family is one of nature's masterpieces," the writer George Santayana said, and I've spent so much time trying to describe what family—united by blood, marriage, or fate—means, without ever defining it so genuinely. I've also never witnessed a family bathing together, and it inspires me to want to *be* more genuine.

To my left is what appears to be a grandmother, rosy-cheeked, ample-breasted, sitting on a low stool next to two younger women who look so much like her, they must be her daughters. And scrubbing *them* are *their* daughters, the youngest maybe eight, the oldest a teenager, and comfortably, nakedly, unselfconsciously, they sit scrubbing each other with firm yet gentle strokes.

And because they do, you get to be part of an agelong ritual of *I care for you while you care for me* that lends a breathtaking intimacy to the room. I believe this custom, if made mandatory for all, could hold the whole threatened world together.

Oh, god, wouldn't that be something?

Now, on the other side of the room, a group of haole tourists (that's exactly what we are called on this island, so I won't sugarcoat it) sit in a hot tub waiting for our number to be called. Once it is, we are escorted to a soaking wet massage table where a Korean woman in a matching bra and panties will scrub us down until there is not one dead cell left atop our raw pink skin.

In a hot tub, it's hard not to overhear, which is usually good for a writer, but this time I wish it wasn't so. The woman closest to me is talking about the defamation lawsuit made by Dominion who is suing Fox News, arguing the company and its networks knowingly made false claims that its voting machines rigged the 2020 election. I'm relieved to hear this, but even so . . . we are *in a hot tub*.

Two other women are behind us in the cool pool, and how they can sit in such frigid water, I have no idea, but the shock doesn't keep them from discussing the even colder topic of data. "Data is not the only place you can find answers, but we've all jumped on the data bandwagon because data is what sells," one of them says. And I think, *wow, that is so true, such an honest thing to say.*

And then I think, *oh, come on, I beg you.*

But it's too late. Like the sun sinking into dusk, my relaxation recedes. And what gets me the most—and this is something I've been wanting to say for so long—is how okay it is with everyone to slide down the rabbit hole of what-is-wrong-with-everything. As if we somehow don't believe we deserve this indulgence, to be happily *here*; that to be accountable first-world women we must suffer the world's woes at all times as if we are personally to blame for all the horrendous acts made on earth, and that guilt is, or should be, our natural state.

I can't help but want the feeling back that I had when I first walked up to the tub, when something in the steamy room had taken over me to remind me how lucky I am to be part of this luscious lusciousness; that something well-deserved would now happen once I took the plunge. Because carrying the world's troubles on our shoulders at all times is the worst stress of all, toxic as poison to our bodies. Life is hard and the world may seem unhinged a lot of the time, but in order to take good care of ourselves, we have to appreciate what is so obviously *good*. I make a silent vow to work harder at not being distracted from what joy there is.

I lean back in the tub, close my eyes, and think back to how, growing up, I didn't get to know my grandmothers in any sort of cozy, confidential way. Certainly not in any stark-naked way. Neither could speak English and they seemed so ancient to me, so strange and otherworldly (their aprons, their bowed legs, their yellowing teeth) that I was sort of afraid of them and mostly stayed to myself whenever we visited their small, dark, apartments in the city. I was only five when one of them died, and shortly after, the other, so I never knew what a close-knit grandmotherly love was.

Until I did.

And when you see a young girl take a loofah to her grandmother's back, it's an act of tenderness that lulls any lingering hard shell to a softer place.

So this is what happened to me in that Honolulu tub: before I could be lulled, before I could soften, I grew annoyed because I can be that way, especially when things seem amiss. I grow impatient because I don't know what to do with some of my emotions a lot of the time other than to let them talk as I try to listen, and it can take a while sometimes.

With my eyes still closed, what I finally learned is that the best thing to come away with from any journey is more acceptance—of the world, of ourselves, of our pasts completely lacking in grandmotherly tenderness (but not tenderness altogether), even of conversations in a hot tub that, at the time, make absolutely no sense at all, but even so, there they are.

And this: we all need attentive, hands-on, affection in our lives.

And I don't mean just a hug, though hugs are great.

We need a scrub, shared with someone we love in a warm, wet, nearly perfect place so that the tubs and nakedness and loofahs and essential oils make you say on the way out the door: Mahalo. Mahalo. Mahalo.

My Greatest Fight

April

Since June 24th, 2022, I can still wake with a start from all the tension churning inside. And it comes on fast, this tension. *Wait*, I cry, *not now. I need sleep!*

Like sirens, these tensions alert me to the truth: it's clear, they have *made* it clear, they intend to govern our bodies.

And in case *I'm* not being clear, I have never been more afraid of Christian Fundamentalism in my life.

Now, saying this in print probably puts me on some data-based enemy list gathered by the Christian Voice, Jerry Falwell's Moral Majority, the Religious Roundtable Council, James Dobson's Focus on the Family, the Free Congress Foundation, and Pat Robertson's Christian Broadcasting Network.

But that's okay. Because they are on mine.

My growing, growing list.

Honestly, I think defeating the ultraconservative right is going to be the greatest fight of my lifetime. (*Not* my softening belly.)

And if that isn't sad enough, I finally got around to watching *The Handmaid's Tale*. The point of the story is to depict how cruel and calculating theocracy can be. I'd put it off for as long as possible. I suppose I was being a scaredy cat about the whole thing, except dread is never benign. But sometimes a film, a book, *reality* comes knocking so hard and it can be just the kick from behind you need to get back in touch with that rallying side of yourself you'd nearly forgotten exists.

Even though you cannot believe we have to go through this again.

It's like stepping back in time.

Or into the future. Reading Margaret Atwood's fore-warning was one thing, but watching rotten men, rotten women, a rotten patriarchal state, well, the possibilities for sleepless nights are now endless.

Almost daily there is another bill to ban something, sponsored by our very own Morality Police posing as rep-resentatives and senators. I try to keep up with all the bans that keep us from paying attention to the important issues, but it's nearly impossible.

To quote my friend Liz, "They are taking away our reproductive rights, they are banning books, guns are now the number one cause of death for children and teens in this country!" And then—because nothing makes her angrier than liberal apathy, so she works really hard to stir it up, and I mean hard—she adds in frustration, "We had an insurrection, people! And you are stressing about your pronouns. For fuck's sake, what's it going to take?"

And don't even get me started on all the restrictive bills in Florida. They are even considering a law that would ban elementary school classrooms from talking about menstrual cycles and other health and sexuality topics before grade six.

Now wait just a minute. I got my period in the *fifth* grade. And it was my homeroom teacher who helped me by accompanying me to the bathroom and giving me all the comfort and instruction I needed. And, believe me, we *talked* about what was happening to me. This did not make her part of any WOKE agenda that legislators like to rattle on about. It made her a compassionate, responsible teacher and mentor.

These feel like such authoritarian times. I'm not sure how many more images I can endure of a man standing at a podium deciding what women can or cannot decide for themselves, while not one of these men stands up to ban automatic assault rifles. And let's be real, American kids are not afraid of women who want final say over their reproductive choices, they are afraid of being shot in the classroom.

I feel exhausted with grief over this new reality.

So much so that lately, when something good happens, when someone does stand up, say, or even spring in the air—daffodils flaring yellow, dogwoods blooming white—I feel like it happens more stunningly in contrast to all the ugly attacks on our rights. My dad would call extremists who wail about denied freedoms while eagerly stripping others of theirs, "goofballs." Which is probably not an acceptable word in some circles, but I think it's perfect, dad. Well said.

One of the fundamentalist's major objectives, of course, is that women relearn the message loud and clear that empowerment isn't ladylike, motherly, or even womanly. This is not only bad for grown women, but also for our girls. We will have to start from scratch to ensure their self-esteem. And it's not just that empowerment of girls and women is still frowned upon by many religious and political factions, it's that when I listen to the ultra-conservative arguments, it is clear that in their eyes, women are still viewed as the domain of men, or the church, or, gasp, *both*. This is what scares me the most.

Even scarier is the role this fear plays in the minds of so many women, and how I sense too many of us holding back what is true about our histories and real about our stories now that certain realities have been deemed "shameful" again. While lobbyists and zealots use our willingness to keep silent to their advantage.

There is nothing more sad than the denial of the truth of our lives.

Regrettably, extremists on both "sides" tend to be the best at being committed and organized. If you have ever felt like you are voting between the lesser of two evils, this is why.

I do gain a bit of hope from the many women coming forward lately with agonizing details of how the Supreme Court's decision put their lives in danger; what they have had to go through. To quote Madeleine Albright: "There is a special place in hell for women who don't help each other." Well then, there must be a special place in heaven for all the women who *do*.

Another ray of hope is Trump's indictments. (This is where I stand up from my desk, walk over to the window, stare at the sky, hope.) My friend Sequoia is a history guru. Really, she bowls me over with her knowledge. "I hear you, sister," she said of my wish that they are finally going to arrest *this* goofball on *some*thing. "Remember, the government was never able to get Al Capone on any of his mob boss murders. They finally nailed him on taxes."

I breathed a sigh of relief.

But I knew this relief could just as easily dissolve. If upholding justice was once intensely in style, I fear it can be just as intensely out of style. Like blue nail polish. Because evil does exist. And it is very fond of social media.

I guess sometimes you just have to turn to Netflix to figure things out. I recently got a text from a friend that said, "Hey!!! Have you watched *The Family*?" There were too many exclamation points after her chirpy "hey" for me to ignore. It's unusual for this friend to send me a text in the first place, so of course I watched the documentary that night. The casualness of texts cannot dull my intuition. I know when my friend has something heavy on her mind.

It was heavy all right.

To learn how sneaky and manipulative men are in the name of Jesus—hosting the National Prayer Breakfast, for starters, which has become *the* hub for backroom, right wing, fundamentalist lobbying—was horrifying. More horrifying is how, when these lobbyists don't get their way about things, like banning gay marriage in this country, they move in and try to win their "battle" in other countries, spending millions to propagate fear of gay people around the world like a gardener sows seeds.

Okay, this may seem like an abrupt change in subject, but bear with me: The other day I was walking down to the ferry thinking about this and that when I was all at once interrupted by what was happening in a doorway on 5th Avenue: Two people, one injecting the other, were kissing. Let me describe some other details about this little scene: while the guy (who looked much older than the girl, with jeans halfway down to his knees, exposing soiled boxer shorts) injected the girl's forearm, he did kiss her, if that's what you'd call it, but he also licked her face like an anxious puppy.

Now, for women on the street, the likelihood of being sexually assaulted is not really a question of *if*, but *when*. I wondered what any of us should do, other than call the police, which a woman standing in the doorway of *Anthropology* promptly did. I say *us* because there were others walking by, but only she and I stopped to notice. The others walked on as if there was nothing out of the ordinary happening on the streets of Seattle.

Which, sadly, is true.

I bring this scene up not because Seattle has been described as a "new Mecca for fentanyl dealers." And

I don't bring it up because downtown is not exactly the emerald of the Emerald City these days. No. I bring this up because when I think of how organized the fundamentalists and the evangelical Right to Lifers have been, I think what a better world this would be if their efforts were targeted at addiction or mental health. Why not make affordable higher education their cause? Or health protection? Gun-violence prevention? Solve a crisis that impacts people struggling beyond hope. Pick something we desperately need and stop picking on women. And please, *please*, start saving children who are already living and terrified of going to school.

I am such a dreamer, I know.

And it's funny, because I've been thinking a lot about growing into the woman I really want to be, and I'm getting there, slowly, even if I don't believe it's ever possible to fully arrive.

It's more like I am a steady maker of headway.

But I can tell you this, at this point in time, I am up to here (my mother would put her level hand under her nose when she said this) with all the righteousness used mainly to shame and evangelize.

Every woman knows control of her body doesn't belong to men who meet in backrooms.

Things you have to steal never do.

One Week

May

Just to be clear, I love what I do. I am so grateful to be a speaker, so appreciative of the programmers who invite me to their clubs and conferences, excited to share my work with willing listeners (six members of a book club or hundreds in a conference room, it doesn't matter), so conscious of the fact that I am doing the work I am meant to do that, as I write this, appreciation fills the room the way air does.

There is no greater feeling.

Even so.

A few events backfire for one reason or another. Times when I have fantasized that if I were the person assigned to hold the door open as the audience members left, I'd let it whack a few of their behinds on their way out the door. (I know I've written about the ups and downs of speaking in public before. But when I say "before," I mean it in two ways, both of them true: I am still rattled by the backfire. And I still need the act of writing to process it.)

No matter what work or meeting draws me downtown, I always take a moment to stop and take in the view of Elliott Bay and give thanks for all that Seattle was, is struggling to be again, and for the beautiful nature that surrounds it either way. Here is the city I know so well. Nearly three decades ago, I came looking for a footing in a promising new city, for a sense of purpose and a place to call my own, never really coming around to the weather, but never happier.

Seattle is not the same city as it was then, and it's especially not the same city as it was before the pandemic. I'm sure people feel this way about wherever they live as we look back—a lot has happened, even more has followed, and it feels like way too much change for some issues, and not nearly enough for others.

So I've been wondering what it is, exactly, that has brought about one change in particular: what often feels like a dwindling, almost a neglect, of public civility. Is it the nearly three years of staying at home? Political tensions? The stress of too many shootings? Putin there, Trumpsters here, crazy régimes everywhere? The constant, repetitive, low-frequency fear of the twenty-four hour news cycle?

Whatever the cause, there seems to be an increasingly less-than-patient attitude toward each other witnessed by a writer who doesn't look down at her phone when she's out and about but pays close attention. To everything.

So much so, I'm not even surprised anymore by some of the bad-mannered, even *mean*, things people say to each other. Latest example: when a woman at the table next to mine in a restaurant on Capitol Hill couldn't figure out how to scan the menu on her phone and asked a waiter for help, he said, and not at all kindly, "I'm not your I.T." and walked away.

Still, one would hope that some people would be better at decorum, especially those who have had every opportunity to practice it. Take one private, prestigious, downtown club. After my last author event there, I thought of someone I haven't thought of in years. She and I were bartenders together in our twenties and we could count on the construction workers and off-shift servers to tip well. But the white-collar guys? Not so much. At least once a shift she would whisper in my ear, "Those with the most tip the least."

Here's what happened: twenty members of said Prestigious Club registered for my talk. Five showed up. The programmer was disappointed. I was disappointed. But that's not the worst of it. Out of the five, four were eating tacos and noticeably intoxicated, two were on time, one bought a book, but only after I sort of embarrassed her into it. At one point, a man dropped his napkin on the floor and interrupted my talk to motion for another, and I remember thinking, *Is there any acceptable way for a female guest speaker to admonish a senior club member who wears a diagonally striped tie?*

And you know I really prepared for that talk. A hometown audience is the hardest, so I didn't sleep well the night before. (It's been suggested I give up red wine in the evening, and I will . . . think about it.) On my way home, I had a feeling of crumbling inside, a sort of identity crisis— *why on earth am I doing this?*

But the yin and yang, dark and light, of being a speaker, of being *alive*, is that the opposite experience is right around the corner.

Sure enough, later in the week I was a keynote speaker for an international organization at a convention center in Scranton, Pennsylvania. I had to travel by air and bus to get there and not just march up Madison pulling a carton of books behind me, but those hundreds of listeners were fully present, attentive, laughed in all the right places, and my book signing went on for hours. They were generous, there is no other word for it. Will I try to emulate their generosity next time I'm part of an audience?

Definitely.

Because for days, just remembering how well that talk went, I felt the best satisfaction. And the feeling lasted for days. In fact, I can still feel it if I close my eyes and remember that room, that podium, those women.

I linger as long as I can inside this memory . . .

A few days later, my new column came out. And while I've never received so many positive emails from readers, a few others didn't like it one bit. It was one of those columns that, line for line, wrote me, eager to free itself. I sat down at 8:30 a.m. and wrote until 4 p.m.

One comment from a reader really got to me: "*I marched the streets of San Francisco for CHOICE in the 1960's, after going through a hell experience in my early twenties when access to abortion meant you had to beg a panel of doctors that you would commit suicide if you remained pregnant. My mother always said, "Abortions would be a nickel on every street corner if men could get pregnant.""*

Others? They'd like to put an end to my voice, to *me*, and told me so.

The oddest thing is how one man begins his threatening emails with "Dear Mary Lou" and signs off with his real name. I didn't want to go to the police. But my husband copied his emails and marched on down to the department.

After his second email, I had a second glass of wine despite earlier advice not to have a second glass of wine. And I let his words go.

Well, I am trying to let them go.

I remind myself that readers' emails are appreciative or horrible. Either way, it's the same writing. When I wrote for the Northwest Life section of *The Seattle Times*, I received my first threat. When I started to write a column for Seattle's Pacific Publishing Newspapers, I received another and I was advised to get a restraining order. I don't want to get a restraining order, but I will if I have to.

So.

Needless to say, it's been a long week.

In the morning, I'm off to Los Angeles.

The last time I spoke in L.A., I was a tad distracted by all of the lip puffing, facial lasering and, oh, the fashion! Fashion that brought to mind a line by Carrie Bradshaw: "I like my money right where I can see it, hanging in my closet."

Other than that, they were wonderful listeners.

Do You Exist Without Your Phone?

July

It's been nearly six years since I replaced my iPhone, and though peer pressure isn't really a thing in my world anymore, I still think there is some of it ahead.

I think this because I just had the battery in my phone replaced for fifty bucks and it now holds a charge as long as it did when it was new from the box.

So why replace it?

The Apple Store Genius (I'm not being facetious, that's what they call the techs on the floor) is my first challenge. He looks at my phone and rolls his eyes.

Oh, god, I think, *here we go.*

While figuring out my syncing problem, he talks with a tone so condescending I feel immobilized, like when an insult comes out of nowhere, or that moment when you realize you've locked your keys inside the car. And here I thought I was a smart, somewhat capable woman.

"Did you just roll your eyes at me?" I say.

Now this guy is trained to look interested, so he tries a bit harder to communicate, but he still looks a little— what's the expression—bored out of his skull.

Whenever a techie treats me this way, as if I am uncool, unintelligent, un*hip*, because I can't communicate at a clip about . . . whatever he is talking about, I just sigh. I want to stand tall, face him, and dance a few moves: plié, arabesque, pas de bourrée. And roll my eyes at *him* when he can't make out which movement is which, say how they interconnect, or pronounce their names. *Pfft, what do you mean you don't know?*

If the age of your phone determines how hip you are, I am hopeless. And if I were to cave to the pressure, it would be me wanting to be hip, which is, of course, the opposite of hip.

It's not like I don't take great joy in my phone. It holds every playlist I use in my dance classes, and I appreciate the brevity of a text when brevity is okay. I also like to catch up on emails when I'm on the ferry so that those thirty minutes slide by as smoothly as the hull.

The hardest part was convincing tech-support that I really didn't want a new phone. Not only am I not taking photos through an ultra-wide lens of every little thing that is happening, or beautiful, or simply *there,* I often feel that I'm the only one not snapping away, and that we have developed into a whole new species of humans altogether, ones who believe we won't survive if we don't record every single detail of our lives.

Which is pretty much what an Apple employee said to me years ago when the iPhone was just starting to appear. I

sat across from him on the Caltrain headed toward Cuper-
tino (Apple's hometown), and that is how he described his
industry's intent: to make us feel as if we literally don't exist
without our phones. "And we'll get there," he said, "one age
group at a time."

I took a deep breath, breathing in as he spoke, breathing out as I tried to imagine what the world would look
like if everyone walked around with a tiny computer in
their hand.

That world looked to me like a world addicted to distrac-
tion, not at all like a world I wanted to live in. I remember
thinking that it would dehumanize our reliance on each
other for company, mess with our self-image, and our
ability to concentrate. That image reeked of anxiety, and it
appeared like an omen on every corner, at every table in a
restaurant, sleeping next to me at night. The omens grew
larger and larger in my head until I finally figured out what
they were trying to tell me.

And today, well, here we are.

When I got off the train, I sat down on a bench, breathless with the idea that one day soon we'd all be willingly
possessed by a phone. How strange, I thought. Why would
people want something like that? How would we carve out
enough alone time to hear our own thoughts, to reflect? I
looked back at the train pulling away and saw that man's
eager eyes, saw my hesitant skepticism, saw my smile that
was fear in disguise, saw a time ahead I didn't quite trust.

Think what you like about prophecies, coincidence,
or chance. To this day I feel as if I was on that train

with someone with whom I was supposed to meet. Just so today, when I look around and see how real Apple's strategy has become, it helps make my uneasiness a little more tolerable.

But hear me on this. There are times when my uneasiness becomes so agitated I need to intervene. I wish I could say I could count in single digits the number of times this has happened . . . but I cannot.

Last Wednesday, when the temperature peaked at eighty-four degrees, I, like many, headed for the beach. If you live in the Northwest, it can be hard to feel exactly when summer begins, but on that day summer arrived with all the luster and sunniness of a Hawaiian holiday. And down where the waves break over the beach pebbles, past the driftwood but before the murky seaweed, there were two girls (maybe twelve or thirteen years of age) who wore bikinis. Bikinis with V-shaped bottoms that made me question if this is what feminism has done for our daughters: brought out their inner exotic dancer.

I couldn't keep my eyes off them. Not because the midafternoon sun had just found us, and everything was suddenly more dazzling. But because the girls were—and you may want to prepare yourself—taking pictures of their bums (to be clear, they were zooming in on each other's butt cracks) in those itty-bitty thongs. I saw how young they were. How vulnerable. I felt as if we were adrift in the world, and I was the only one who could save them.

From themselves. I walked up (my husband says I ran) and asked them to please, *please*, think twice before posting those images. That "teach your daughter that her mind should be the most beautiful part of her" line certainly played loud in my head. But so did, "It takes a village." Though what I was really hearing is, "It takes the women of a village to run this kind of interference."

It almost frightened me to feel so maternal, so driven by concern. Maybe I should have just turned away and let YouTube/TikTok/Snapchat/Instagram have its way with them.

But how could I?

I am not willing to "mind my own business" (which, predictably, is what one of the girls promptly told me to do) when concern comes on this strong, especially the part of me that can't bear to imagine the men who would view these images.

I know that interfering like this just might be too pushy of me—jeez, today it could get me shot—and that maybe I should have just brought my phone to the beach, sat on a rock and texted people miles away instead of noticing the ones right in front of me.

But honestly, I wouldn't even know how to begin to do that.

I realize this may be keeping me from adjusting to our world and accepting it as it is.

So, maybe the key is simply to admit what is true: I *am* so unhip.

Threads

August

It's a familiar story: I met someone who became my friend. And though this someone was a man, we were never more than a friendship. From his first dance class in my studio to his last, there was something between us that might have made people think we were more, but it was never like that.

I remember the first time we talked, really talked. We leaned against the barre with our arms folded, our thoughts freed, and from then on our conversations ranged from crucial issues (personal history, politics, good choices we've made but just as often bad) to the everyday (films, books, the absurdities of small town life). "That woman," I said to him once, upset about a comment made by the graphic designer working on my book cover, "had the nerve to tell me that I dressed too stylishly for a small town. What kind of an artist would say that?"

"Someone ought to tell that woman not to walk around in yoga pants," he said. "Her backside looks like a mattress

folded in half." I loved him for saying the words, for rushing to my defense, for being a man who could deliver a
line like that without apology. I found it freeing to laugh
with someone whose sense of humor seemed to mirror my
own. He always did know how to make me laugh.

We laughed about so many things.

And when he got cancer, once or twice we even tried to
laugh about *that,* but it fell flat. Frantically, I kept working
on a piece of choreography. I thought by trying to capture
what was coming, I could handle it, which right there is
the worst self-deception. Whatever I thought I knew about
coping at the time, I had no ability to admit that the choreography may have been a creative try at managing fear,
but it wasn't working.

Meanwhile, he got weaker.

If there is one sink hole you never want to go down, it's
this one: I started to read everything online about cancer.
But what those websites never tell you is that the only way
to deal with grief is to, first, surrender to its intensity—
which is like the seven major plates of earth shifting inside
you—and secondly, take all the time you have left to love
others as much as you can. There are so many people in
need of so much love.

The year after he was gone, when I struggled the most,
it felt as if the future held far fewer protections than I was
used to, as if part of me believed that if I reached for any
sort of safety net, I'd fall through the mesh. I still feel a
loneliness so deep when I look at a framed photo of him
dressed as Othello that sits on a shelf in my living room.

But we are capable of bearing the unbearable, of moving on—an absurd phrase when you think about it, as if we are idle while grieving—and so we do.

Or no. That's not how it feels. It's more like we come back to ourselves.

Eventually.

But not exactly as the person we were before. Words I couldn't have said when my friend was dying but just now they easily wrote themselves.

And today, when I drive from my home on Bainbridge Island to teach dance in Port Townsend, I give myself extra time to stop in Chimacum because that's where he lived. I thought I'd have to avoid this route, but that's not at all how it is. I like to shop at the farm store that sits by the four-corner stop, but mostly I want to get out of the car, stand, stretch, and breathe in the air that surrounds a place he loved.

Maybe we use metaphors because they are such a reliable writing tool. Or maybe we use them because they help visualize what we are trying to say. I like most the ones that deal with something painful while also trying to lessen the pain, and when I walk by the yarn store on the ground floor of my building near the ferry terminal with its window full of colorful skeins, I can't help but compare weaving to the complexities of, well, *us*. The fact that two threads need to bind in order to interweave is just so metaphorically *perfect*.

And out of all the perfect metaphors, this one stands out for me: I was bound to him. And in many ways, I'm still at loose ends without him.

But in other ways, I'm stronger. The strength I've gained may feel more like a knot than a knit at times, but the point is it *holds*. And though I'd like to say this hold comes from having known him, that's not the whole story. A large part of it comes from finding the courage to let him know me.

Every time you let someone in, you are taking a risk.

This is the line I say to myself every time I reread this piece from the beginning to this point.

I think it is trying to tell me to end right here.

On Manitou Beach

October

Around this time of year, when gardens sag; when stakes and strings hold up what's overgrown—and much of it is—it's the last of the cherry tomatoes that remind me how I could live without squash or pumpkins, but I could never live without tomatoes. Tomatoes sliced and sprinkled with olive oil and salt, absolutely, but my favorite way to eat them is right off the vine. The taste is a mix of late summer and fall and rivals anything sweet I have ever eaten.

When you compare this taste to the grocery store version, bred not for flavor but for packing and shipping, it's like one is a true love story and the other makes me think of faces that don't know how to smile anymore. Just sadness. Not a single happy expression.

When my dad built our family home, he planted the tomato garden before he laid the foundation, making it clear that tomatoes are essential to day-to-day life. The next year he added cucumbers and peppers, but they never had priority over his tomatoes. When I asked him why he planted the garden behind the garage instead of behind the kitchen, he told me he didn't want to feel—*feel* rather than hear—all the noise that goes on in there. This was my first understanding of some basic things: That sound will bounce off of us in much the same way that light will reflect. That a garden ensures alone time. And that by planting his feet in the dirt, my dad always seemed to cheer himself up.

But no matter how long he spent in the garden, it was the sun, water, and soil that reigned, and I came to see how relinquishing to nature relaxed him more than anything. At work, even at home, he was a control freak. But in the garden, he could trust that nature would take care of things.

Yesterday, I was reminded of something else essential to Italians.

It was a revelation. (Another revelation!)

And if anything demonstrates how we continue to learn about ourselves, it's a revelation.

This one took place on Manitou Beach, a twenty minute bicycle ride from my home. It was there I met another Italian woman, lucky for me. She was beautiful, and her looks and hand movements were pure Italian.

Naturally, we got to talking. In superlatives, at first— *You are?! So am I! I thought so!* In no time, we launched into real conversation. She exuded the kind of attentive directness I seldom meet in anyone, much less on an isolated beach on an island, and it took only minutes for me to realize that what made her so much fun to talk to was that she kept interrupting me and I, breathless with joy, kept interrupting her and nothing about it felt rude or impolite. When I pointed this out, she reminded me that in Italian culture, it would be rude to *not* interrupt, "It would seem like you weren't paying close attention," she said.

It's been so long since I've shared a meal with my extended family, that I've nearly forgotten how we'd sit around the table for hours, talking, arguing, interrupting each other, no one thinking they had to hold themselves back to be polite. Disagreeing, interjecting, and how you handle both, is all part of the intuitive mix. Like hard work, it's meant to relieve tension.

"So," she says, "it can be hard here sometimes."

This is true.

"Because remember, immigrants from Nordic countries settled the Pacific Northwest and Nordics tend not to interrupt each other. They will save their input until you have finished speaking. And we live right next to Norwegian Poulsbo. So, you know, *waaaay* different culture."

On my bike ride home I thought about how this was by far the most interesting thing I've heard about my background in a long time. It made me wonder if we have any real control over who we are. I don't mean to make a habit of interrupting people (more than I already do), but I like the idea that my interrupting stems from heredity. I like the implication of it—enthusiasm rather than rudeness.

The best part of this revelation was that I realized how grounding the conversation was for me. There is something mysterious about a serendipitous revelation no matter where or when it occurs, something even bet-ter about being just two out of millions of Italians who found each other by chance, if only to better appreciate a particular trait about ourselves. And I suddenly had this overwhelming feeling that maybe we don't transplant all that well. No matter how cold and gray spring was in New England, maybe all those little Dixie cups full of tomato seedlings helped my dad feel warmer and more connected to the country he missed so much.

Now, my husband is a mix of Scottish and English. And if you Google what Scottish/English conversational traits share in common, you will find this: "They like to engage in polite conversations. It is best not to inquire about personal information upon meeting them." Reading this, I had to laugh, because if my husband had been with us on the beach yesterday, once the woman and I started to talk, I'm pretty sure he would have walked on down to the sand to inspect the seaweed. Years ago, before I put my foot down, and I do mean *down*, he would hold his hand up as if directing traffic if he even suspected I might interrupt. He is not breathless with joy, ever (unless he is imitating me), and nowhere in his conversations are the emotions that brought him to his opinion unless I beg him to elaborate. Even then, it will take him twenty-four to thirty-six hours to figure out what he thinks he thinks he maybe thinks, but he's not really sure. And you can just forget about how he *feels*.

Before this chance encounter, I was beginning to wonder if there was something wrong with me to care so much about what is being said that I just can't help but interrupt. Which, in these parts, is generally perceived as So Damn Rude.

When I called my Italian friend who gives tours of Italy during the spring, to tell her about my revelation, she said in a way that sounded removed, and yet very personal, "All these people want to rent a villa in Tuscany and tramp all over Rick Steves' version of Italy, but what they really learn about Italians you'd have to multiply by a hundred and then we'd still have only the beginning of any real understanding between us. Also, I think," and then she hesitated, but only for a sec, "they pay attention too little and eat too much."

As I reread this story for the umpteenth time, it's easy to see how writing is a lot like gardening, and I am a lot like my father: I tend to my work methodically, the process relaxes me, and eventually I have to relinquish control.

And the fact that the next time I just *have* to interrupt someone, I will no longer feel like a very bad person, cheers me up no end.

The Monsters Among Us

November

Yesterday was a gray, drizzly day, a chilly reminder of the months ahead.

But today is one of those clear fall days after the rain, when the air is filled with a charged anything-is-possible atmosphere.

For as long as I can remember, I've been fascinated by this season. As the last leaves cling, I like to remember what the biologist Merlin Sheldrake said: If we pay close attention to the life hidden under the leaves, it may reveal something about what is going on under the surface of *us*.

I don't know if this is true, but I like to think so.

Because the truth is I feel a little lost lately. Too many things feel overwhelming: world leaders who would rather bomb women and children than talk; presidential polls; AI hiring more and more people to figure out how employers can hire fewer and fewer of us (and why I will continue to use human cashiers). You name it.

I take a deep breath.

Whenever I feel this way, a walk helps. Once out-side, any illusion that I can control much of anything is dispelled. You probably have your own take on what calm-ness is, but to me, a walk offers the best of it. I pretty much always end up feeling better than when I set out. When I think of some of the toughest decisions I've had to make in life, what comes to mind are the walks that helped me see my way. Nature is the globe, we are inside of it, and rustling leaves is one of the most peaceful sounds.

Until the monsters arrive.

They come in a deafening roar, powerful enough to blast from street to sidewalk to lawn; filling the air with the stench of gasoline, reminding us that perfect peace is like a perfect world.

It doesn't exist.

I compare leaf blowers to gasoline-powered termites, decimating a log in no time.

Except this comparison is unfair to termites. Termites are as much a part of nature as leaves and roots. Leaf blowers are not. They are the most infuriating of all the infuriating tools of the lawn-care industry, as well as the best yardstick of my emotional state. Whatever worry lies suppressed is sure to surface as soon as one of them is fired up within hearing range.

Why are we so troubled by nature's perfect mulch made of chlorophyll and light?

Sadly, nearly everything about how we "care" for our lawns is harmful. Pesticides poison the insects that feed the birds. Store bought mulch, piled too deep, smothers ground-nesting insects. But gasoline-powered leaf blowers make up an environmental hell all their own, spewing nitrous oxides and hydrocarbons—not to mention pollen, mold, animal feces, and chemicals.

Why do we stand for it?

Some things remind us that we can't complain about something if we don't try to change it ourselves. Maybe, like soft soaps and dryer sheets, we just didn't know how toxic everyday items had become.

But once we do know, what then?

The desire to quickly clean a walkway is understandable; stubbornness to not replace a gasoline model for a quieter, battery powered one, less so. The newer battery blowers may be less powerful, but when you think about the fact that the gas-powered model was originally invented by a German engineer in 1900 as a flamethrower that was used by the German Army in 1911 and subsequently by other armies, including our own, well, isn't this sort of what it sounds like today? That we are at war with our yards, overpowering rather than nurturing?

The other day I cycled past a man who was blowing a single leaf across a driveway. I knew he wasn't doing this to annoy me knowingly or consciously. I slowed my pace and thought, *Why not just bend over and pick up the leaf?*

Despite the noise, the squirrels kept at it. A good lesson in silent acceptance.

But to be honest, I am really bad at it. I have no patience for gasoline-powered leaf blowers. None. "Please stop," I yelled, but not as loud as I could have. Actually, it was probably the first time I'd responded so politely to such a challenging noise. He gave me a look and then revved his machine, the leaf-blower equivalent of giving me the finger. One block away, another guy raked his yard as if the effort was one of life's primal pleasures. I blew him a kiss.

Eager to include another opinion here, the least I could do is ask someone else how they feel about gasoline-fueled leaf blowers. I thought long and hard about who I should ask, not wanting to sound like someone who thought she was entitled to ban leaf-blowers simply because *she* doesn't like them.

I wound up asking a man in the paint and stain aisle at Ace Hardware, probably in his mid-fifties. He was a little bemused at first. Then he said, "I guess they're sort of like letting crazy guys run for president. Not enough of us got off our butts to say this is really nuts and we should stop."

"Oh, that's perfect," I said, thinking how concern about the 2024 elections are already starting to fizz under the surface of a lot of us.

He smiled.

I left the store with a smile on my face, too. And I'm thinking he went home and said, "Some woman asked me about leaf-blowers today . . . "

December

December

On an otherwise overcast morning in December, the sun peeps out.

I love the sun. I feel lighter in its presence. It spills through the branches of a huge horse chestnut tree that grows on the property I live on. And it delivers.

It always delivers.

It delivers so much I don't want to go back inside. A few of my neighbors make cameo appearances, but only one stays as long as I do. She peers up at the sun with one hand shielding her eyes, turns to me—but only partially, so as not to exclude the sun from her line of vision—and says, "I love this time of year."

I know she thinks of winter as "cozy" and "peaceful," but I don't share her enthusiasm for it. Of everyone I know, she'd do best if forced to live in a tiny cabin in Alaska. Last week the temperatures were brutal. When she went for her walk in freezing temps, I said that sounded better than going to the gym, but I knew I wasn't going to follow through. I waved from my little balcony and scooted back inside. She got what she wanted and so did I. I remember literally jumping up and down, I was so happy to be back indoors.

But not to worry, the sun will soon deliver springtime, too. When I say as much to her, she corrects me, saying, "It's been spring-like all week, really."

Which is just so annoying.

This all makes me think of how certain things—sunlight, seasons, bubbly neighbors—are really more than good comparisons to life, they *are* life. For example: Life is like a rose: beautiful and prickly. My mom used to say that. And this: Winter will end. It always does. But I can hardly believe I just turned my new manuscript over to the editors; that three years and two months of work has also come to an end.

I *can't* believe it.

Because this means I'm between once more.

Between this book and whatever is next.

And as I've made known in previous writings, I have trouble with this interlude.

Lately, I've started to compare myself to a border collie, but only to people who own dogs. "I need something to chase after," I'll say, "I don't like having nothing to do," and they'll smile and nod, a bit surprised, but happy I can talk about dogs even though I don't have one.

But honestly, I think I'm more like a cat, getting what I need by digging in and not letting go.

A lot of people will tell you this isn't good for you, that

you should "chill out," but I don't agree with this senti-
ment. I understand what they mean—because sometimes
it shows on my face, or they can hear it in my voice—but
not all stress is bad stress. There are parts, acute attentive-
ness for one, that I like bearing down on my brain. Stress
that fights for space among all the tedium is like sunlight
itself. I really can't get enough.

I might have said the exact same thing about stress
before I understood how intrinsic it is to any creative process. Before I knew how to handle it or how to contain it. I
like to believe I wouldn't have said this to someone before
I got all this, but I think I must have.

Before I figure out What's Next, I like to think back on
what I've gained and lost in the three years and two months
since I started this book: The best thing is that Larry and I
found a new home on Bainbridge Island. After losing our
downtown Seattle neighborhood—or what felt like losing
it—I went searching for a home that didn't break my heart.

By far the worst thing is that my nephew, Jonathan,
passed away, suddenly and much too young.

Sadly, my dad can't remember his own name any longer,
but the last time I visited, a gentle nurse combed his hair
and sang to him, and he all but purred. I have to believe he
is in good hands, or I'll go mad.

One friend drifted away, another I sort of cut loose (no
more friends who talk like they want to set me straight, I
don't need setting . . . or straightening), one of my dear-
est friends died (grief is such hard work), and my three
bests still love me, or maybe I should say they tolerate

me lovingly (and I love them so much it makes my heart spring when their names come up on my phone). And several new friends have come into my life. One makes me happy in ways that make me feel giddy with good fortune. Another, well, I don't always get her sense of humor, but I laugh anyway because her drollness is never like, oh, god, shoot me now. I don't want just people anymore, I want souls to match.

I'm still happily married to the man I met at nineteen (I picture him reading this, how the realization that we've been together forever might hit him as he thinks to himself—hopefully—*I would pull over to the side of the road and pick her up all over again.*) I was hitchhiking up to the Sol Duc Hot Springs. He drove the shabbiest VW van I'd ever seen. I didn't hold it against him. As soon as he jumped out of the driver's seat to ask where I was headed, I knew. I also knew what was going to happen in that van the moment I set eyes on him.

One thing did lead to another.

My publisher said yes to publishing another book, this book. What a great idea!

And holy crap, I was invited to teach dance in Pape'etē in Tahiti, and I thought it might be too much to fit in during a launch year. But then I thought, too bad, I'm going.

Oh, and this might not be part of the same gain/lost list but I'm on a roll: While swimming a channel in Hawaii I've swam for twenty years, my leg got nipped by a baby reef shark. "Baby" in that it was only, maybe, three feet long. "Nipped" in that it was light compared to a serious bite.

It was the perfect storm of events, one any swimmer in my swimming tribe can relate to: I left for my swim without eating as much as I should have, and because the current was strong, I depleted fast. When I got to Kaimana Beach, the water fountain wasn't working, so because I couldn't swim the full distance back without hydrating, I had to cut around a rock levy where anyone who has spent time in the water off Kaimana knows the whitetips like to nestle in and sleep. When I swam too close, one of the babies sort of rolled over and gave my leg a little nip, like, "Hey, get out of my cradle!" A warning, but hardly an attack.

All sharks have the ability to learn and adapt. Maybe it recognized me.

Plus, whitetips are not aggressive. They are not tiger sharks. I've seen only one tiger shark in all my years of swimming in Hawaii, some fifty feet away, and I still lose sleep over that sighting. I slammed the whitetip hard with my fist and swam off. Fast. When I saw my friend Ellen treading water near shore and showed her my bloody leg, she said I was in shock, took me by the hand, and walked me home. I was in the water the next day. I had to be. Life can be scary, but we (I) must continue to take risks for happiness. Different people need different things to be happy, and I need to swim. I can feel the scar if I rub my fingers over it. It's a little discolored rise. You can hardly see it anymore.

So, big adjustments each: an island reprieve, unexplainable deaths, fluid friends and those solid as a rock, a nurse who cares, that first phase of love, fish that bite—everything seemed to flow together somehow, old roots growing deeper, new growth shooting up, and here we are.

I mostly write non-fiction, so I don't see closure as a real thing. An easy tool for fiction, maybe, coupled with our need to label everything, even things as complex as emotions. In reality, we just face the next challenge.

My biggest challenge is what to write next.

Something will come to me.

2024

January & February

A few favorites from earlier collections, revisited. They are a culmination of all the things that made me happy about writing when I was new to the genre of essay writing, in much the same way they do now.

Family Reunion

I can only write about my family reunion in hindsight. The reasons for going are obvious, but initially I resisted, staring at my invitation, then hiding it from view.

But as the world shifts under our feet, the personal effect is even greater: A feral-like need to connect with those we love.

Upon arriving, I am stunned by the contrast of past and present. I am transfixed. Emails and Christmas cards are one thing, but family in the *flesh*, that's quite another. I am so happy to be with people who look and talk like me that I almost burst into tears.

The affinity I feel is overwhelming; I am bowled over by affection, by the wide open idea of family itself.

So much so that writer-eavesdropper that I am, I start to scribble notes on a cocktail napkin. But instead of feeling like a writer, I feel like a spy. Not the sister, daughter, cousin, niece, and aunt I need to be between breath-catching silences.

I confess, since losing our mother, I've remained close to my sister, but I see less of my dad than I like. And it's been twenty years since I returned to the fold of my *extended* family. Twenty years! Living in the Northwest can do this to an East Coast transplant. I still have a clear mental picture of me all those years ago, Jordache-jeaned and riding a Greyhound bus across the country, leaving home not a decision I needed to mull over. From early on, I sensed that in order to find out who I was, I would need to shed, mile by mile, who I was not. And when the bus had gone as far west as possible, I hopped off and found a place to re-root.

My life opened to the Pacific.

And opened again.

Yet, there is no denying that the faces filling the reunion suite belong to the proud people who were there for me before our roads forked. And with each stride I take across the carpeted room, my world pauses, like a good listener, to let me move into my family's orbit without hesitation, embarrassment, or any of the other flustering emotions that define the wandering, restless will of an immigrant's daughter.

Which brings me back to why, sitting around a table in a Manhattan supper club where photos of Frank Sinatra and Joe DiMaggio hang in gilded frames over the bar, I am reminded just how far I've strayed. Because, though I wear my best dress from Banana Republic, to the women of my family, unless your clothing has sequins, you are *not* dressed up. And when Cousin Johnny actually says "bada-bing" for emphasis, I laugh out loud. Worse, when he stands by the door with his chin up and arms crossed behind him looking like a bouncer hired for our reunion, I joke that he reminds me of Tony Soprano. This is where he shoots me a look with those thick black eyebrows to let me know that we are simpatico, but I'd better put a lid on it. Then he hugs me, lifting me right out of my heels. From that point on, we are cousins again.

But only after I nod to a second round of antipasto am I fully trusted. Because he is not, I soon discover, anywhere near amenable enough to consider the word "vegetarian."

I don't let this bother me. To my family, food is tantamount to faith, and you don't stray from its consecrated dictum. This might be my body, but it is their Holy Eucharist.

But don't a lot of my friends define a huge part of themselves by what they will or will not eat? Isn't there usually some food politics to contend with in the company of those of us who feel entitled to our likes and dislikes no matter what? No matter how contradictory?

Recently, at one of those B&B breakfast tables that make me cringe (I am not a morning person. I am especially not a morning person who likes to sit with strangers at 8 a.m. and make small talk), when the vegan sitting across from me spoke out in support of the Native American right to slaughter another magnificent whale, I had to challenge her convictions no matter how many times my husband kicked me under the table. And when I invited a friend from Los Angeles to dinner, she emailed me a list of what she will not eat.

Mentally, I compare this to my family's food issues at hand: Whether a pound of pasta per person is enough to serve. How, as soon as lunch is over, conversation shifts to supper.

I don't even try to give my family a view of Seattle they can identify with. A city that can feel, especially during local elections, as segregated as the deep South. Not by race, but by ideology. Or how its people eagerly espouse cultures other than their own as if searching for an identity (think Tibetan prayer flags snapping over Scandinavian foyers) and how this differs from my family's way of embracing only their own culture. How does one begin to describe a city with less of an ethnic culture and more of an all-encompassing attitude that encourages a near desensitizing sensitivity, to people who have never viewed conversation as a tool to think hypothetically? I'm aware of my family's provincialism, but when you get right down to it, is there any real difference between meditation crystals and rosary beads if peace of mind is all you are after?

When I first went away to college, I remember hanging a sign on my door that read YOU ARE NOT YOUR FAMILY! But everything I've discovered since is that OH YES I AM! In ways I can choose to carry forward, ways I can try to let go of, and in ways I cannot adjust the alignment of no matter how much I try.

And so, to my great surprise (and as exhausted as it made me), I climbed back up the rungs of my family tree.

And what did I learn?

That I *can* turn a new leaf into one far more flexible. Which defies any rigid idea I might have had about autonomy. Because family, however you define it, asks us to reach a little higher, do something more, make the extra effort.

And today it's hard to tell which is better—the effort or the outcome.

Letter To Rose

Rose, your email came at just the right time.

Because here it is December, and I'm at a loss. What can I possibly say that captures the spirit? Everything "holiday" has been written before. I have my doubts as to whether I can find a fresh angle.

When you become a writer, Rose, you'll understand, I promise.

Before I forget, your saying that you read my column is the best present. How many fifteen-year-old girls even read the paper? Which makes your gift even more precious. Sure, your mom and I know each other. Still, knowing her, knowing *you*, I infer no female in your home is deciding what the other female reads, period.

What I need to tell you, readers, is that Rose wants to be a writer. But when she shared this with one of her teachers, she did not get the reaction she was hoping for. In Rose's words, "I'm told I need a backup plan."

Rose, trying to do the jigsaw of maturing is no easy feat for any young person. But, trust me, if you have already found work that makes you happy, a huge piece of you will not go missing. I will go so far as to say that your writing may turn out to be your truest friend in life. This might not be an easy thing to hear in your BFF world, but no friend, especially no boyfriend (doubly hard, sorry), will be able to fill that place inside of you that longs for so much.

Only you can fill it. And writing will help.

But, boy, I was thrown into a tizzy after reading your email. See, in the seventh grade, I called my home-economics teacher by my English teacher's name and in front of my classmates, she yelled, "Mary Lou, get your head out of the clouds! Pay attention!"

I was mortified.

I imagined not suffering in silence but walking right up to her desk and slicing her head off the rest of her body, like when two yams are conjoined, one smaller than the other, and all it takes is a single swipe to make the smaller one go rolling across the counter.

How could I have explained to her that I *was* paying attention. Or that I knew how important names are to people, I'm just bad at remembering them. But ask me anything, anything at all, about what she was wearing, the ever-changing color of her hair, her squiggly crow's feet, the little lines around her mouth filled with coral-colored lipstick (scary to a teenager), or the single hair growing out of a mole above her upper lip, and I knew, baby, I knew. I was obsessed with the details. Noticing was my skill in the world, I just didn't know how to apply it yet. I didn't know how to make use of the fact that not only could I remember, specify, describe, perceive, elaborate, but I loved doing so. But to retrieve someone's name unless I know them well, honestly, to this day, I go blank. I soak up the visual, but I'm resistant to first names the way some people are to colds.

I'm porous to forenames. They leave me. I'm a sieve.

And surnames? Forget it.

Rose, just think how much time I could have saved if my teachers or my guidance counselor had picked up on my wordy, descriptive babbles (I had a proven reputation for them) and leaned me toward creative writing instead of laying the secretary/nurse option on so thick. Insecure, vulnerable me might have left high school with a feeling of *I'm going to be a writer*! Instead of the vague *I have no clue what I want to do* feeling that made me face my future with phony confidence, while my insides knew better.

See, the thing about my guidance counselor, the thing about my guidance counselor and *me*, is when I look back at the two of us sitting in her office with fifteen minutes for concerned-looking her to study my file and make a stab at my future, all I could see was what she was *really* able to help me with, which was ... absolutely nothing, that's what. Rose, what you have to understand is that I knew that the person before me, a full-fledged member of the adult working world, was going to be of no help whatsoever.

Here's what she said to me, "You can make more money as a secretary. But nursing offers better benefits to your family."

Benefits? Family? Death to a seventeen year old.

Funny, she said nothing about teaching, which is what she did before becoming a counselor. And she certainly said nothing that helped me perceive my individualities as the very traits a writer needs. Gradually, through the years, I learned this on my own.

High school, for me, bristles with so many of these memories.

But not to worry. In time, all the lost little parts of me came together, together enough anyway (there are still plenty of gaps), to make me see how I really had no choice about what I was meant to do in this life because I was already doing it.

Just as you are.

It's not hard to see how the rest of my life fell into place around me in all the determined, shared-by-writers, obsessive ways it needed to: notebooks full of ideas, pages and pages circulating and rejected and rejected, rewritten and then published, some of them. Every surface of my home well-thought-out and tidy because I thought if I could keep my place clean and well organized, I could keep my goals in order, too.

By the way, I still believe this.

As the world around me grew more daunting, in other words, as I grew older, I sat for longer and longer intervals, trying to make sense of it all, or some of it, any of it. Which, when I think about it, especially as a college freshman, was way better than drugs and alcohol, or dividing a tomato into a day's worth of calories.

So, Rose, I advise you to keep following the swerving stretch of road onto your very next page.

Above all, promise me, promise *yourself*, that you will be totally and completely selfish about making time for your own work. Remember the word "selfish" is rarely applied to self-disciplined men. And be open. There will be possibilities that will come along that you never envisioned. Don't pass them up.

And more than anything, Rose, more than anything in the world, insist on passion.

Love Is All You Need

"So-oo? You and your husband are a love marriage?" my new friend, Amargit, asked. Amargit is from India where families still arrange most marriages.

I didn't know how to respond. She said, "Ye-es?" before I could. She seemed a little nervous about my "love marriage." She *felt* a little nervous.

I felt a little uncomfortable.

I didn't want to tell her, or not yet, that I'd met my husband while hitchhiking Highway 101. He pulled over and, quite literally, picked me up.

I think back to that question, how she viewed me with such wonder, how I paused, and in my hesitation I realized we were taking our first leap of faith. In an instant, we both recognized how we didn't quite register reality in the same way and how, if we were to become friends, we'd need to jump from two very different points across a vast cultural divide.

So that's what we did. We jumped.

Being who I am, though, it didn't feel like a jump, it felt more like being curious in a city where 40 percent of the foreign-born tech employees are from India.

At first, we'd smile through the awkward silences, make our way back carefully, dive back into conversation that didn't ask too much of us, not even close to the kidding around we manage now. We just had to learn to let go of the carefulness that made us hold back some of our questions and too much of our*selves*, as we struggled to share the everyday in an everyday way.

So, before I could put romantic love into words for her, I was busy asking myself if I should say something funny? No. Serious, then? No, again. Elaboration wouldn't do. It was a simple question in need of a simple answer. "That's right," I said, finally. "A love marriage," and because I couldn't stop myself, I started to sing, *all you need is love, love. Love is all you need.*

Tilting her head to the right, she responded, "Ye-es?" lengthening the sound into two syllables again, making more of a serious question out of the word and, though not intentionally, more of a clown out of me.

Funny, funny me.

My stomach flip-flopped.

Humor can be the most difficult disconnect between cultures, it really can. Even now, years later, mine often goes missing somewhere in the silent space between us.

Luckily, with no reluctance—none—Amargit moved us onto safer ground. "You have a beautiful voice, ye-es?"

Honestly, if diplomacy could speak, it just had.

It was Super Bowl Sunday when we met at Macy's downtown. (I miss that store. I miss willing myself, sometimes successfully, not to linger in front of the shoes. Or the handbags. Or the jewelry bling always on sale, before taking the escalator up to the second floor lounge.) I was shopping for nothing, really, just strolling through the empty aisles to clear my head. Amargit was working, rearranging clothes on a rack. "You don't like football?" she said, grinning. And when she pronounced her name, I repeated it, barely audibly, pretending to grasp the sound, straining to remember it.

From the start, we intrigued each other. She wanted to learn more about the freedoms of American women now that she is one (I like to remind her), and slowly, over the years, we've chipped away at the bulk of our differences, only to find that underneath we are just two women who want to talk, laugh, grumble, share.

Talk. Laugh. Grumble. Share.

There is something more I want to say about these four words: they are the definition of intimacy. If lucky, we find it in a friendship. If really lucky, in marriage.

Finally came a big, big day for Amargit and me. She and her husband, Tito, invited my love marriage, Larry and me, for dinner at their home on their one day off a week (*if* they take it). They and their two college-age sons (their education the reason the family immigrated) live in an immaculate apartment north of the city. As soon as I entered, I wondered if maybe this is why she'd hesitated inviting me here, needing time to be sure I'm not the kind of person who'd snub someone who lives in a two-room basement apartment off Aurora.

That night I was shocked to learn something else Amargit hadn't disclosed. In India she didn't need to work. By

Indian standards, she had plenty of money. She employed several "house servants" (I admit, I gasped) who slept on bedrolls in a corner of her home, waiting on her family's every need. Which all sounds very un-Seattle-PC, I know, but what better example of how much she wanted to ensure an education for her sons. And now they, Amargit and Tito, husband and wife, work six, seven days a week waiting on others.

The feast Amargit spread out for us that evening remains one of the eating peaks of my life. Naturally, we got to talking. Which led to a story about how Tito removed his turban and cut his hair the first day on American soil, a ponytail that, since boyhood, wound around his head several times underneath his headdress. How relieved he felt. "I was freed from religious and cultural law," he said, "and much cooler." We laughed. "Life is more fair in America."

Ah, yes it is.

Here is where I could have said how unfair it is that he still won't allow Amargit to go anywhere alone, other than to work. Nowhere with me, certainly, not without him or my husband tagging along. And what fun is that? (Just kidding!)

But I decided not to wave my Independent-American-Woman flag so soon. Though I detect a bit of mellowing on his part. His younger son's girlfriend joined us, a beautiful Afghan student who proudly told us that, yes, she can date without chaperones, making clear how, in a single generation, everything can change.

She also told us how she, her parents, and six sisters left Afghanistan.

"Did you flee? I asked.

"Oh yes," she said. "We took an airplane."

"No, I mean from us, the Americans?"

"Oh yes. There were many bombs."

Another bomb, of course, was my nervous laughter. But she was warm, relaxed, not offended. Bless her for that. And later when I baptized Tito "old-fashioned," he laughed. "Ye-es," he said. "I am very ancient."

Funny. Originally from a family of immigrants, I fought my whole life to get away from such old world traditions.

And then the years went by.

Choices, choices, choices.

And here I am in a new city facing all the same issues, relearning my way around.

All the more wiser. I hope.

Clara-fied

For as long as I can remember, I've been wanting to write about Clara Rhodefer. I've been putting it off for over a decade because, for one thing, my fondest memory of her has to do with watering my vegetable garden, and I haven't watered a vegetable garden in far too long.

For another, I didn't want to write a story about Clara while she was still alive. Clara was a very private person.

My husband and I used to rent a cabin from Clara. Her property, better known in Sequim as The Old Rhodefer Farm, has a large white prosperous-looking farmhouse that Clara lived in. It overlooks the rest of the land, including the tiny cabin *we* lived in. One month we came up short of cash and Clara suggested we paint the cabin in lieu of rent.

About a week later, with scaffolding strewn all over the yard, Larry and I stood staring at our freshly painted home, Clara joining us for once. She'd pretty much ignored us until then. She lived in the main house for eighty years and I guess she felt she should have a say in whatever goes on next door, even about the beans I planted, and I noticed she kept looking down at them instead of at the cabin. Placing her hands on her hips, she looked directly at my pole beans and said, "Well, from here they don't look so bad."

How many people would say such a thing? It endeared her to me.

Only her frankness was nothing compared to the approval I felt when she finally walked over to stand with us. I felt our out-of-town-ness was finally being accepted. That *we* were finally being accepted. I stepped closer to her. I often know in a second the people I want to be closer to.

She looked at me crossly. "Mary Lou, there's something I've been meaning to tell you."

"Really? What?" I braced myself. Larry put his hand on my shoulder.

In her no-nonsense voice she said, "You should water your garden in the morning while the ground is still cool so the roots can handle the cold water."

Was it true?

It didn't matter. What mattered was that she wanted to share her knowledge. Farming know-how has been in Clara's family since Seattle was a logging camp, and everyone has a desire to share what they know with someone who'll listen. I'm the same way about writing. There's almost nothing I don't want to share about the truths of a writing life.

So I listened.

But I wasn't totally convinced, so I said the first thing

that popped into my head, "I thought it was better to water in the evening after the sun goes down so . . ." I had to think for a minute, "so the water doesn't evaporate in the heat of the day."

"No, cold water distresses roots that are still warm from the sun."

So I said the next thing that popped into my head, "Larry told me to water in the evening."

It was one of the many, many times I have believed someone simply because that someone was a man. I don't know why we make these errors in judgment when we are young women. But we do.

Larry looks at me, realizes I have blamed him, and says, "Hey, what do I know?"

This made Clara laugh. From then on, I was happy to take Clara's advice. As instructed, the next morning I watered first thing.

"You've been Clara-fied," Larry said.

By the end of August, I had to lift the hose way over my head to reach all of my vegetables. When the spray hit, it made a splattering sound, so I'd adjust the nozzle to a softer mist. I'd look up and see Clara reading the Gazette at her kitchen table, but I knew she was watching me out of the corner of her eye.

Neighbors can teach you a lot. Like how we are really so clueless a lot of the time, that we learn when we are open to knowledge, that we should always put learning first even about things small and inconsequential, and if we do, everything else will follow.

But the best thing Clara taught me is how watering is a great way to start the day.

The best.

For plants and for people.

Empty Nest

I t seems that I'm in a period of loss right now.
No one close to me has died or anything, but for the last year, I've spent nearly every waking moment rewriting the last draft of my first memoir.

Memoir. Such a word.

It's as if I've been writing about some other woman, a younger woman, who lived not so long ago on one hand. Eons ago on the other.

Then I sent her away.

That's it. Years of work zipped through cyberspace to my editor.

In my head I got up, ran outside and twirled with my arms like Julie Andrews in *The Sound of Music*. In reality, I just sat there not knowing what to do. Or how to feel. *How should I feel?*

I suddenly couldn't believe how empty I felt, how light of head, how much I wanted to call the pages back. There was nothing to do now but wait.

Waiting is the worst part.

I straightened up my desk, brushed off the keyboard, swabbed between the keys with a Q-tip; that's how lost I felt. I remember feeling that if I were a color, I'd be a streak of lipstick smeared past the lips, out of sorts, out of place.

This is the period of time that slices me in half, when I'm nowhere near my best self, like when a book is in its infancy and I'm scared, absolutely, but all that fades as soon as I begin.

Half of me feels like I need all the focus and discipline in order to survive.

The other half is quite happy to live without that kind of pressure. She fears the only place she knows herself well is cloistered in her office. She needs a break from all that, to disconnect for a while, to kiss her work good-bye.

I can't even fathom how the book pulled off writing itself in the first place. Every writer says the same thing, "I have no memory of writing the book whatsoever." It's as if the harder we work, the less memory we have of working at all. Where our minds go in the long hours of writing is anyone's guess.

And now?

I get a couple of weeks, three if I'm lucky, to add a little spaciousness to my days, partly because I won't feel the weight of a deadline hanging over my head, and partly because I won't be living an intense dance life and an intense writing life at the same time. It's been great, but I feel a need to separate my writing time from dance commitments.

I will remind myself of this every few days.

And then the email I both await and dread pops up. The subject line reads, if a little indifferently: CORRECTIONS/ AMONG FRIENDS/SANELLI. I lean forward. There is a crucial decision to be made: Open it? Don't?

You would think that because I've been through this process many times, I'd know how to handle the stress better.

Unfortunately, no. Fear is not a feeling you ever get used to.

I stand. Walk away from my desk. Stare outside. To let off steam, I curse under my breath at the man blowing leaves. Does anyone but me miss the soothing, swishing sound of a rake and broom? My relationship with the leaf-blower (both man and machine) is a horrible one.

I clomp back to my office, sit, tap my fingers, inhale, exhale, clear my throat, before finally, resignedly, clicking onto the attachment, every page filled with red lines, dots, arrows that will rip me open, first with glaring RED-ness, then with comments I will, and will surely *not*, agree with, which may explain why I am, and will always be, in awe of good editors.

But before all this, before I can even get this far, I will think, *No, sorry, I can't do this.*

I will even shout "I can't do this!" so loudly it will travel through our home and scare my husband, causing him to come running before he sits to listen as I go into overdrive, explaining why I'm convinced whatever I wrote is crap and that coming too close to it all over again will cause me to crumble inside, that I don't deserve to be a writer, that

I'm not worthy, that I can't do it, I can't do battle again. It will kill me.

Until I, taker of risks, go over the text again.

From the top. Page by page.

I read somewhere that courage is like a starfish. It regrows.

Well, it's true. Most of my writing life has been spent waiting for my nerve to regenerate.

Which gives me plenty of time to perfect the way I will myself not to overreact when someone asks me what I do and when I say, "I'm a writer," they tell me how much *fun* it must be to be a writer. Before they say something like, "Actually, I have a little book I work on now and again. I'm somewhat of a writer myself."

A *little* book? *Somewhat* of a writer? I don't understand.

"Really?" I'll say, "good for you." But what I'm thinking is how much I envy Joanne, my dentist. No one says to Joanne, "You know, I do a little dentistry on the side. I'm somewhat of a dentist myself."

Oh! Would you listen to me?

Here is where I'm going to change tack and "count my blessings," as my mother likes to say.

Because my work really is going "great guns" (another mom-ism). In fact, if I stop to think about it, the email from my editor was so positive, it made me feel as though I could write forever. And when the process works like this, there is no better feeling in the world.

I should end here, on a "positive vibe" as my friend Diane would say, but I just have to tell you that other times it feels as if I'm incapable of finding my way back to real conversation with real people and, worse, unable to separate my writing brain from my conversational one. Because both keep asking me the same questions: Am I grateful that writing is my life? Or is it a curse, all this reflecting? If I'd known when I began what I know now, exactly what being a writer demands, how poorly it pays, the stresses and burdens, the isolation, self-esteem nearing and departing (and so willingly), would I have become a writer at all? Should I continue working on the Next Book that is already trying to sweet-talk me or move on to things in life that are lighter, that don't demand so much of me?

This has got to be what it feels like to leave your youngest at the bus stop for the first time or your oldest at college for the last.

Any way you slice it, it's an empty nest.

I carry on. I sweep. I dust. I wipe down the kitchen counters again. (Here is where my husband would add that I'm finding him all kinds of extra chores to do.) I sit on my balcony bundled in a blanket, watch the sun slide onto the cedar tops in the orangey way it does this time of year.

It's been a crazy couple of months. I've never been so up and down.

Thank goodness my subconscious took over to remind me that lousy things are going to happen in life, in my career, in general. And my job as a woman, a writer, a wife, a friend, is to enjoy the ride anyway. "It's all about the ride," she will say.

Then—noticing, I'm sure, the neediness in my eyes, because moving another book into the world will not include much of the thing I deserve: money—she will add, I know she will: *Remember, you write for another reason, a reason that stays with you long after you've blown your wad, so, please, don't torment yourself about money. It will crush you. And it bores me to tears. And while you're at it, think about what the cost of having work you love is worth. Who could afford to pay you such an exorbitant price anyway?*

Gratefully, I won't have an answer to that.

Afterword

The other day, while signing copies of my last book, a woman asked me a question. "Do you define yourself more as a writer or as a speaker?" She paused. "They have such different effects."

"On my readers or me?" I said, without blinking.

Over the years, I've learned to deflect any question that catches me unawares at a book signing table, and this was a question I'd never been asked before.

Book signings are like that.

Someone is always asking a question when it's hard to say what I really think because I'm distracted. But the woman exuded a sort of pure inquisitiveness. Pure interest, too. So, I decided it would be better not to answer, but to consider the question at a later time, sit on it, think about it. Until afterward.

For my afterword, I thought. *Perfect.*

I'm a writer. I'm a writer while always trying to become a better person. Which, I believe, makes me a better writer. That's a huge part of who I am.

Still, I don't think it *defines* me.

I'm fairly certain that the closest I can come to any such definition—though it describes my way of thinking more than my entire being—is to compare my mind to the split screen monitors above my husband's desk. On the left screen is whatever I'm working on, while on the right side is everything else I need to do in a day, a mental list of what I enjoy, have promised, or feel responsible for. When concentrating on the left, the right screen glows in the background, impatiently, but it dims enough to let me write my pages for the day. When I finally give my attention to the right screen, the left screen fades. Slowly. Reluctantly.

That I would come to combine my love of words with my love of bringing my words to life, this I can put squarely at the feet of my first dance teacher. He had a way of moving. His motion would spill out in all directions at once, transforming our studio into an elegant stage, generally in the first five minutes of class. He embodied the promise of grace and lasting fitness, and he never let us feel like either was out of our reach, no matter how clunky our own movements were.

Whatever he said, we listened.

Still, speaking is a social act. It's only when you are alone with an author's work that you can feel the full weight and intimacy of the writing.

As for any effect my writing has, all that matters is that it has an effect at all, that my readers are stirred in some way. Other than that, I am constantly on alert to keep all thoughts of effect at bay. "Que Sera, Sera," as the saying goes. Anything else would feel like something close to pandering, and I just couldn't reconcile that with the writer I want to be. Suppressing what someone else might think or say, or tuning out the critical voices (imagined or real) has become an integral part of the freedom I long for as a writer.

But to be clear, I am a writer *because* of these voices. In the beginning, I often gave my power away to people in the industry who, quite frankly, didn't have a clue. It became foremost for me to learn how to write because a part of me believed what too many critics want you to believe: that you can't; *that I couldn't.*

Today, if one of these voices, tsk-tsking away, objects to my way of writing my truth, and for a brief moment I think about changing what I'm about to say to appease it, I remain absolutely still for a few seconds with my eyes closed, until the voice recedes, and I think *this is me, this is me being me*, and I am safe again in the relief of trusting myself.

And this relief is like the sun when it brightens into a golden radiance just before dusk sets in.

To me, the best time of day.

Acknowledgments

As always, this book was made possible by the encouragement and support of so many people.

Thank you to all of the hard workers at Chatwin Books for your untiring work and effort. This book would not have been conceivable without you. You have been the perfect home for me, you help me every step of the way. I am deeply grateful to Phil Bevis, editor-in-chief and publisher. I am just about as much "do something, anything to fix it," as he can stand sometimes but even so, he has always given me steadfast support. To Molli Corcoran, our Marketing Director, for giving so much, so often. I am entirely grateful. To Anna Brunner because editing and proofreading are their own form of a miracle; I thank you for your knowledge, time, and impeccable eye for detail. And Ryan Long, you help me tremendously. When I arrive somewhere to speak, my books are neatly wrapped and patiently waiting. I am indebted to you. And to Diane Rigoli who has designed many of my books with such brilliance, thank you. You are much appreciated for your deft design skill as well as your friendship. And let me just say if you are going to publish a book, you need a great team around you and the book designer is a major part of that.

I owe so much to my readers, to *you*. Sometimes I feel you know as much about my life as I do. And because so many of you have taken precious time to write to me, I want you to know that your support has encouraged me from my first book until now. Also, I want to thank all of my friends who have had to listen to me go on and on about "my new book" in the most joyous stages of its development and the most difficult. I owe you so much in every real and affectionate way. You remind me to keep laughing at life. And at myself.

I have changed the names of some people to protect their privacy.

The 2024 writings appeared originally in earlier collections, in slightly different form. They pointed me in the right direction and gave me confidence in the path I was following. I am grateful that I was able to record them for local public radio, as well as for NPR's *Weekend Edition*. The others have first been published in: *The Seattle Times*; The *Kitsap Sun*; Pacific Publishing Newspapers: *Queen Anne/Magnolia News; Madison Park Times; L'Italo Americano; We The Italians; Yahoo News; Bainbridge Islander; Art Access; Lilipoh* Magazine; *The Seattle Star; Adelaide Literary Magazine.*

One last thing: Throughout the writing, editing, and publishing of this book, Larry has been wonderfully supportive. He never complained, at least not to me, when

I spent many weekends making sure every page, every word, every detail, was just right. And though I'm sure I still missed something and that there is still more to do in that regard, I think I'll take a break now. Really, I will. Let up a little. Maybe even cook dinner. I promise.

Printed in the USA
CPSIA information can be obtained
at www.ICGtesting.com
LVHW020513200824
788520LV00002B/5

9 781633 981751